C.P

TRACTS AGAINST THE TIMES

TRACTS
AGAINST
THE TIMES

DAVID MARTIN

LUTTERWORTH PRESS

GUILDFORD AND LONDON

First published in Great Britain 1973

ISBN 0 7188 2040 1

Copyright © 1973 David Martin

*Printed in Great Britain
by W & J Mackay Limited, Chatham*

FOR

Jonathan Paul   Jessica

Izaak David   Magnus Aidan

Sources and Acknowledgements

The essays brought together here derive from a number of sources and I wish both to indicate these and thank those who have given permission to reprint.

The principal essay on 'R. D. Laing' comes from M. Cranston (ed.) *The New Left* published by the Bodley Head in 1970 and reprinted in *Dissent* in June 1971. The other essay on Laing's work concerning the family was printed in *Encounter* (February 1972). I am also most grateful to *Encounter* for allowing me to reprint 'Red, White and Black' (February 1970), here retitled 'Black Papers and White Immigrants'. 'Trouble in the University' was originally a broadcast talk printed in *The Listener* (March 7, 1968) and 'The Nursery of Revolution' was printed in *The Spectator* (January 31, 1969). 'The End of the Protestant Ethic' was printed in both *Freedom at Issue* (March 1971) and *The Director* (December 1970). 'Young Men Seeing Visions' is reprinted by courtesy of *The Christian Century* (September 1970). 'The Wronged Box' (here retitled 'The Image Breakers') is reprinted by courtesy of *The Times Literary Supplement* (November 6, 1970). Thanks are due to Routledge and Kegan Paul for 'The Dissolution of the Monasteries' in the book I edited with the title *Anarchy and Culture* (1969).

Contents

1. Introduction

THIS collection of essays and reviews requires some preliminary explanation and autobiographical background. Their genesis is fairly clear: as the crisis mounted in British universities a member of the sociology department in the most famous institution affected by the troubles was often called on to write on events, to explain what he thought was happening and to review the works of radical ideologues as they impinged on the scholarly fields which interested him. I perhaps found myself in this role more often than most because I was concerned with religion and the religious aspects of the so-called 'revolution' have frequently been remarked upon. Indeed, many people in the churches have either been cheered by this revival of religiosity and by what they took to be the existential concern of the revivalists, or else been pioneers of radicalism within the churches themselves. My first direct acquaintance with the ideas and attitudes now familiar on the student left was through the churches at least three years before they rocked British universities. So both in terms of the place where I worked and my particular interests I was closely engaged by the phenomena of radicalism. Further than that, my initial concerns as an academic had been with the thirties, and especially with its anarchistic, pacifistic, Marxoid fringe, and the late sixties seemed in part a repeat performance of that time on a wider scale.[1] Few academics can hope for a historical déjà vu of their special interests carried out on their own doorstep.

It will be obvious that I am not a sympathetic observer, partly because the radical ideologues have wrecked a case that ought to have been made. They have revived religiosity in its most irrational forms, defended personal identity by attempting to eliminate its sources in stabilities, structures and continuities, and attacked the quantifying and crassly empirical wing of science by denying the

[1] D. A. Martin, *Pacifism. A Historical and Sociological Study*, (1965).

very idea of knowledge. Their assault on privilege has in *actual practice* amounted to little more than an extension of their own privileges at other people's expense and their penchant for openness has in its social manifestations resulted in repetitious denunciations of all those who disagreed with them. In other words they are antipathetic to the objects of a university: rationality, knowledge, discussion. The rhetoric of choice, of equality and of a wider definition of knowledge has been self-defeating, and has curved round against itself in a celebration of relativity relieved by constant declarations of faith. Perhaps this was inevitable: the collapse of the march of reason in history and the appalling consequences of old-style Marxist revolution in the neo-Puritan mode left little option but a mélange of personalism, anarchism, vitalism and intimations of alienation.

But this anticipates the substance of the book. My sympathies were originally with them. I didn't realize that reasonable requests would mount a continuous escalator of unreason, or that the focus of demands would shift not only from one topic to another but veer from one fashionable extreme to its exact opposite. Above all, one was on the one hand being asked to look after them as if they were children and on the other told that they were a generation for whom paternalism was out. It was all very well being treated as a human equal marked off only by the criteria of experience and knowledge, but few people have a vocation to be fathers whose role is defined as the corrupt slaves of their righteous sons. All men are corrupt, and the doctrine that the sons have been uniquely exempted is not a plausible piece of theology.

Naturally, one was led to ask about the social soils in which such a mixture of fervent anathema and of salvation by faith rather than by knowledge might grow. Progressive education was an easy object of suspicion; too easy in fact. Indeed, in a rather different form, this theory suggested that the fathers were indeed the corrupt agents responsible for the diseases suffered by their children. And it is in any case not pleasant to suppose that the advances in educational theory of the last few years contained seeds of disintegration. Clearly to join in the criticism of progressive education would expose one to allies one was not used to having.

Nevertheless, when there is a war on, even a war of cultural styles, one cannot be choosy about allies, or reject every genuine criticism of 'progressivism' merely because it has also been latched onto by 'the wrong people'. Nor can one worry too much about having to accept labels like 'authoritarian'. War, *especially* war over cultural styles, is a matter of labels and propaganda. One can only note that those who label one in this way claim themselves to be averse above all to labels.

Many of one's allies in the universities were not at all objectionable and it was at least interesting that some of them joined their defence of the classic humanism of the university (and of the 'Protestant Ethic' on which it rests) with a deepening mistrust of some developments of educational theory. Neither they nor I were in favour of mindless regurgitation, passive acceptance, grammar at the expense of meaning, rules at the expense of substance. We were in favour merely of ordered accumulation as a more satisfying mode of learning than random osmosis. We found ourselves saying that both rational growth and personal identity rested on a base provided by rules and that rules were necessary short-cuts and not bars to creativity.[2]

The most obvious allies in this battle for ordered educational advance were those who had benefited from the last instalments of such advance: the group Richard Hoggart called 'the scholarship boys'. These found themselves in collision with middle class radicals whose knowledge of progressive education was derived from experiences of élite schools working under specially favourable circumstances and whose knowledge of state schools was nil. In the view of those who had received the benefits of a good state education the ideas of middle class radicals were disintegrating standards of excellence which they had learnt, sometimes painfully, to appreciate. The consequence was clear: their children now in state schools were too often in receipt of an education markedly inferior to their own. Moreover, because that education was supposed to leave so much to personal choice, it in fact left everything to the standards of whatever culture a child happened to be

[2] cf. Bernice Martin 'Progressive Education versus the Working Class' (*The Critical Quarterly*, Winter 1971).

in, whether this was provided by a deprived home or a philistine peer group or by the automatic donations of the mass media. My own son, initially in a 'collapsed' comprehensive school, suffered the depredations of the peer group and the media and was saved only by the fact that our home is not 'deprived'.[3]

There was thus a profoundly reactionary consequence to progressive education linked to a psychological disorientation closely related to the attack on the very nature of a university. This link was perceived not only by those who desired to defend rationality but also by the proponents of subjectivism. The 'radicals' saw the importance of subverting both school and university simultaneously, and extended their attack to the family and the Church. Every structure of sequence, cumulation, rite and role has been attacked as a constriction of existential freedom. Hence the counter-attacks made in the following pages on such ideologues of radical psychiatry as Ronald Laing. The defence of role and rite in the Church I've conducted elsewhere in a published correspondence with Professor Gordon Rupp. But wherever it is to be found one needs to point out the deeply anti-human consequences of a movement whose overt intention is the extension of freedom. Rarely has the gap between proclaimed intention and observed consequence been so wide. A defence of order is rendered even more difficult when serious discussion is subverted by the influence of media pundits devoted to the indiscriminate rhetoric of self-fulfilment and by the impact of the imagistic, disintegrated mode which dominates media presentation. Hence the short essay on 'The Wronged Box' originally written for *The Times Literary Supplement*.

From what I've said about the religiose nature of the radical movement it should be clear that most of the essays which follow are implicit contributions to the secularization debate. This debate concerns the supposed demise of religion in modern society, and my own contribution elsewhere has endeavoured to stress both the irreligion of many periods in the past and the rampant religiosity

[3] Only after four years of subjection to the principled disorganization of ignorance did we move him to a comprehensive school with a firm notion of its own standards. Since then he has prospered.

INTRODUCTION

which can sometimes be found in the present.

The forms of contemporary religiosity are many, some overtly Christian, some related at some removes to Christian sectarianism and mysticism, some embodying free-floating items originally embedded in Christian theology, some exploiting the resources of various oriental mysticisms. Most of them have an indirect affiliation to the radical wing of the Reformation and to the antinomian consequences which can be derived from the dogma of salvation by faith.[4] Dr. Laing for example veers between a Calvinistic sense of total reprobation and a radical antinomianism. Jeffrey Nuttall on the other hand veers between celebration of rural innocents dancing round a phallus and a clear statement of Christian mysticism: 'You can't dig It if you *are* It'. Dr. Roger Poole constructs a mythology of subversion in which the imagery and structure derives from the New Testament without endorsing a theology of any kind. Professor O'Neill speaks of the resurrection of the body in terms which represent the theology of William Blake translated for moderns. Yet others, Timothy Leary for example, instigate ecstacies which are far removed from the disciplines of occidental mysticism, or indeed the ascesis of most oriental mysticism. And in all this the overlap between the academic counter-culture and 'pop' culture is fairly clear. There is common object of attack: the Protestant ethic of work and duty, the devotion to an objective external truth and submission to the dictates of logic.[5] In short, science is under pressure whether as the study of 'the given' in society or the given in the natural world. Contemporary religion rejects science and scientia-knowledge. Its only subject is the self.

All this represents a theology of the self, for which discipline of the emotions or of the reason, or the imposition of external discipline and academic disciplines is anathema. The discussion of 'Order and Rule' criticizes this ideology of the masterless self just as the essay on 'The End of the Protestant Ethic' attempts to describe it. The problem for the secularization thesis is precisely this: the Protestant ethic, rooted in order, discipline and cumulation

[4] cf. the essay entitled 'The Dissolution of the Monasteries'.
[5] cf. the essay entitled 'The End of the Protestant Ethic'.

13

is subverted by the Protestant dogmas of salvation by faith and 'experience'. In an analogous way empiricism is being undermined by experientialism. The structures of word and ecclesia are corroded by mystical invocations of images and by groupings which are based on the temporary and haphazard overlap of visions. I don't believe these are universal phenomena of modern society but they pose a problem for those who maintain that one defining mark of modernism is secularity. Whether the Church as traditionally understood will survive in such a welter of religious experience is another matter, but I have decided to conclude with an essay on that topic. After all, there is a double question mark: the survival of the Church and the survival of secularity. I desire both.

NOTE:

Many of the above points can be found stated from the radical side by Paul Goodman, especially in his 'New Reformation' (1970). I have attempted a critique of Goodman's form of Jeffersonian anarchism in 'An appreciation of Paul Goodman' (New Statesman, June 1973).

2. Trouble in the University

This was the first piece I wrote on student troubles and it occurred in response to an invitation to contribute, in February 1968, to 'Personal View' on the B.B.C. Third Programme. At that time the troubles were very recent and discussion of them highly speculative. My own speculations concerned the socially mobile student who glimpsed the humanist life-style but was denied full access. I still think this is one of the patterns involved though research suggests that the typical student rebel tends to be a product of the professional liberal middle class. The piece retains a margin of sympathy with student aims and ideals which experience was later to erode.

There is trouble in the university. Students here and there are rebellious, ancient ideals are questioned and the academics are under pressure. In Germany the students have been overturning tramcars and arousing *bürgerlich* hostility by marching through Berlin. The other day the French police had to disperse students in Nantes who were demonstrating against discipline in halls of residence. Last week, following last year's disturbances, there appeared the Report on the Machinery of Government at the LSE in which a student minority claimed near parity of power in almost everything relating to the university. And the *Times's* second leader commented that to concede anything like this would be a betrayal of academic responsibility.

The activist minority of students claim a large say in what and how they are taught, and who shall teach them. Some academics even find themselves defending their right to mark examinations rather than hand them over to the vote of intellectual workers' councils. We have not yet reached the situation of some late Medieval Italian universities, where professors asked students' permission to marry, but the inexorable march of progress may well bring that golden time round again. There is even an 'anti-university of London' where antibodies meet and antitheses are written. If I take some of my material from my immediate environment that is because it represents certain tendencies in an advanced form: no student has been killed, as in Western Germany, no rector besieged, as in Istanbul, but for a laggard Britain the L.S.E. is the pace-maker.

There and elsewhere, practitioners of rival disciplines have singled out the sociologists as one cause of the trouble. It is not for me – as a sociologist – to comment on such opinions, but to suggest how sociology may be used to tell us things about a much wider student population whose nuisance value is much publicized but whose personal and social difficulties are not widely understood. A particular subject and a particular place is only important because it makes articulate what many other students feel, because it gathers together in a large suppurating boil what is otherwise dispersed in the system. Sociology is less the cause of student unrest than a vocabulary in which unrest can express itself. It does not create deviants so much as give them opportunity to locate themselves. And it is above all the upwardly mobile male student from the working class or lower middle class who needs to locate himself. Sociology provides an ideological home and the L.S.E. a physical habitat. No doubt membership of a minority group can frequently add to his burdens. Hence the talent for alienation as well as the yearning for community.

It is not much help to say: 'They knew what they were coming to when they came up.' The point is that they did not. For all I know, they thought St. Clement Dane's was the college chapel, that Sir Sydney Caine daily recited Latin grace from high table and that one of the delights of London was a quiet dream-like punt under Waterloo Bridge. Or maybe they thought that Lionel Robbins wrote for *Tribune*, the governing board was composed of journalists from the *New Statesman* and you could get hold of Sir Karl Popper for a quiet chat about historicism almost any evening in the Three Tuns bar. Who is to know what they thought or what wild aspirations failed to find satisfaction? One thing only is certain: they did not know what to expect, because they were ignorant.

A combination of ignorance and severe stress ought to attract compassion. Compare the situation of the first or second-generation migrant into the university with that of the long-established scion of the middle class or upper middle class, going up to Oxford or Cambridge. For the latter, his home, university and profession are relatively all of a piece and the period at university is often more a *rite de passage* than the crucial phase in the determination of his future. It would hardly have mattered too much if education had finished at 18. But for the migrant the university seems the only door to his future, and his performance while at university can appear the final rating given him by society. He cannot even feel that being a decent fellow is better than being an academic success. Moreover, home, university and work are three universes in collision and the migrant is himself the point of contact. Mostly he survives the explosion, of course, coping as best he may, working hard, entering his profession and so on. What I say applies only to a minority, even in my own subject.

The public schoolboy may pride himself on being a good fellow, a thrusting leader, an exemplar of good manners or a fine sportsman. The immobile working-class boy can live within a world of limited aspiration and judge his successes and deprivations on a restricted scale of reference. But what of those who have great expectations? For them there is only social and political righteousness. Consider the situation of migrants, and the reaction of this articulate group to it. So far as migrant engineers and natural scientists are concerned, there is some continuity with their previous schooling: they have often been taught to know rather than to think, and much acquaintance with the humanities is hardly required of them. Their range of intellectual reference is narrow, or at any rate restricted to areas which do not reflect their personal life or social problems and which do not activate dormant queries about the individual or society. For these students the future is assured and they probably do not feel that the university is a glimpse into a different life-style from which they are mostly barred entry. For the others, however, the future is less sure and

17

the subjects taken bound up with a particular life-style, broadly that of the humanist intelligentsia.

Outside Oxford and Cambridge this style is often only dimly apprehended as a vague threat; enough is imbibed to break, and break brutally, the umbilical cord with home, but not enough for entry. Moreover, this dim apprehension exaggerates the pleasures of academic existence: the leisure is, after all, much more apparent than real and the academic role much afflicted by tensions between teaching, research, necessary conferences, administration and contacts. Hence the occasional unavailability of teachers, and the fact that this appears to students as intentional neglect. I'm not saying, of course, that neglect is never intentional.

This is an old theme of the displaced person but the contemporary student extemporization on it shows some significant variations. Students appear to be a potential élite and are indeed often referred to as such. Some even see themselves in this way: 'We are the country's future', said one, 'so they dare not do anything to us.' To the ordinary citizen they seem to have been given privileges and entered into a land flowing with intellectual milk and honey: yet to them it is as hospitable as the Gaza Strip.

Why do they feel so deprived? It is somewhat paradoxical that the genuinely deprived in our society are not much bothered by it, whereas the relatively privileged seethe with discontent. The genuine proletariat is often profoundly conservative while part of the student élite can posture in the proletarian role. The working class is insular; the migrant to the middle class is inclined to link his little local difficulties with the cause of truth and justice the world over. To hear some students talk, one would have thought the battle of Vietnam was being won on the playing-fields of Houghton Street, that Black Power and student power were all of a piece. Or, as one young woman summed it up, 'there are three great issues in our time – Vietnam, Rhodesia and the L.S.E.'

Righteousness is not only an attitude but requires a social alignment, a location, and it is here that the proletarian identification is so useful as a bridge between adolescence and adulthood. No country satisfies this need for a heavenly home, not even China, but a mythical proletariat can: it provides security, and a platform independent of both school and university. It asserts a permanent and incorruptible political virginity hiding behind the apparently sophisticated clothes of a mysterious radical vocabulary and sociological analysis. One can be contemptuous both of the simple prejudices or aspiring hopes of home and the corruptions of the academic world. One can even claim that those corruptions have twisted the minds of one's mentors, so that one is being forced to imbibe the poisoned fruits of bourgeois thinking. Such a view can have additional attractions for those whose capacity for imbibing is not very great anyway. You go on to conclude your mentors are human – a surprising notion which had hardly occurred to you before but now gives once-revered teachers all the status of dethroned gods. As a student pamphlet put the matter, the sit-in has revealed them as just ordinary human beings. It makes you wonder what indeed they expected when they first arrived. No wonder the university was a disappointment.

The theme of incorruptibility takes some curious forms and arouses many a corrupt response. Take the don who handed one young Robespierre a copy of *Country Life* in return for a copy of *Agitator*. Yet the truth is that some students are so anxious for mobility they dare not admit it even to themselves: hence nothing disgusts them so much as ambition and the rat-race. And indeed, if you cannot be too sure of making it, there is something to be said for not even trying. No doubt there is here an understandable objection to the competitive aspects of our society, but it is curious the way some radicals simultaneously posture in the part of a proletariat, full of deep vital solidarity and full of the righteous zeal of 'we shall overcome,' and still complain they are not promoted fast enough. Incidentally, for those who have not played it, there is no game as boring as 'prolier than thou.'

When all your father figures have failed you, or rather when your new fathers-in-academia have destroyed your old domestic gods, without immediately grasping you to their bosoms, you are chronically unable to enter into a career structure, sensitive to even the slightest suggestion of hierarchy. Hence you may either enter a profession bearing a grudge that you are not immediately translated to the very top, or suffer a kind of permanent adolescence as a perpetual student. At least part of the urge to post-graduate work finds its motivation here: the desire to form a modern *vagantes*, to embrace life-long intellectual vagrancy. Hence it is not surprising that some of those who curse the university most furiously and criticize its imperfections in the bitterest terms also beat most imperiously on its doors to be allowed another two years of identical misery. When asked about this apparent contradiction, one replied: 'Yes, it is a poverty-stricken place, but it's the best there is.' In fact, it is no exaggeration to say that you have a situation where some people are shouting: 'Let me in, let me in immediately, or I will never ask you to let me in again.'

Of course, the group suffering most in all this is the lower middle class: disliked by the insiders and the outsiders alike. I recollect advice given when I came up to university: 'If you are working-class you can be brash, if middle-class you can be eccentric, but if you are lower-middle-class you will just have to be correct.' The lower middle class and, for that matter, those going from commercial backgrounds to destinations in the commercial professions are largely correct: neither original, nor magnificently untutored and splendidly raw. They have their own righteousness, of course, of the kind that is held up for satire on a programme like Talkback, where businessmen and social workers appear together in a common defence of decency which makes NW1, or rather NW3, heel over with uncontrollable merriment. No doubt it has come to something when a diet of *soi-disant* student radicalism leads one to feel the Talkback people have a point after all.

Yet this is an attitude which must be resisted. I have rarely, in fact, found students individually unpleasant, however deranged they appear when reciting their pieces for each other's benefit in public meetings or resting their feet on the amenities they claim do not exist. Their situation is genuinely ambiguous and difficult and it is not remotely surprising that a few become badly upset and disorientated. Their enthusiasms have a genuine element: only the other day it expressed itself in a large collection for the victims of the trawling disasters. We get nowhere by saying that we don't have the right type at university these days or suggesting that 20 per cent ought not to be at a university at all.

This type of confusion over status has frequently produced political and religious radicalism in the past, and the present furore has elements of both, not merely Marx but anarchism, Existentialism, Buddhism, not to mention deserializers, detotalizers, dereifiers, deobjectifiers and repersonalizers. One sectarian enthusiast asked me what I was going to do in the 'post-bureaucratic age'. Another threatened me with the coming time when they would appoint professors by some combination of workers' control and a gallup poll. Yet another shouted, 'You are in chains,' as if he were a modern Praise-God Barebones.

I mentioned just now the game of 'prolier than thou'. If there is one game even more boring it is called 'dressing by the left'. This is only played among the virtuosi and is a contest in purity. One man establishes himself as the true diviner of the 'real' proletarian viewpoint. He then has to maintain his position as the genuine incorruptible one by looking over his left shoulder to make sure nobody else is there. All positions to the right, of course, are opportunist and what happens in that direction does not matter, but once let somebody stand on your left and your position crumbles. The main rule of the game is therefore: never be caught in a compromising position. I have suggested that no on-going political system corresponds to this position, certainly not the Soviet Union, which arouses unmitigated contempt, especially from the protagonists of the Kronstadt rebellion. But I may be wrong: for the genuine adherent of the 'Pure Land' sect there remains Cuba. Hence periodic pilgrimages to that happy country.

I suppose we require endless patience, without pretending we take their more extreme attitudes seriously. Maybe we also need to suppress the reaction that suggests we can give them nothing just because they ask for the moon. I don't think either that all will be easygoing if they are given more representation or relieved of disciplinary action. In any case, the institutions most bothered by the troubles are conspicuous for the laxity or non-existence of discipline. But we do need to induct them into the kind of independent existence which they associate with adulthood and are so unwilling to endure in practice. If they were independent, they would depend less on their teachers: would be less inclined to demand our instant availability. We must help them to impose their own structure, especially on their time. We must learn to teach and teach them to learn.

One indication of their immaturity is the demand we should tell them the Truth as distinct from more or less verifiable truths: we ought, I think, to be much more tender to such a demand. We begin by instilling habits of criticism and scepticism towards the conventional wisdom without considering what a vacuum we can create in their minds. Unfortunately, we have no rituals to fill, even in part, the gaps left by evanescent faiths. I don't mean that academics have no faiths but, when hard-won over the years, they are not so easily passed on in a few lapidary phrases or in the shibboleths of a self-conscious nonconformity. They believe we are hiding something from them and that locked up in our drawers are the Eight Noble Truths which whosoever shall know shall be saved.

Perhaps part of this is due to the schools, though it is not necessarily their fault. I don't hide my conviction that far too many of our schools are well-organized conspiracies for the suppression of intelligence. At any rate, students need some preliminary introduction, not to particular techniques but to systematic thinking, particularly about their social environment. So far as the university is concerned, I believe we have given up ritual much too easily. Give up the solemnity of the common meal, give up high table, and the result is meaningless cafeteria in separate dining-rooms. Hierarchy and order there must be, but not separation. And however much you abuse the re-creations of Oxbridge, the units of organization are not too large and the rituals do solemnly guard the fact of community. Speaking of rituals, we ought to write to Canon Collins a letter of congratulation on the revival of C.N.D. In the halcyon days of C.N.D. they could work some of it off on the Long March, and suppose their troubles were due to a Conservative government. Alas that they should be disillusioned about that! We could also institute an old-fashioned rag but when it comes to a choice between the kind of student who pours flour over policemen and the political student, I much prefer the latter.

3. The Dissolution of the Monasteries

The essay below formed the introduction to a book on Anarchy and
Culture *(1969) which I edited for Routledge and Kegan Paul. Initially I
was asked to collect a group of essays on the theme of violence, which was
then attracting quite a lot of attention. But on reflection I felt the central
issues turned around the role of the university in a society with developed
bureaucracy, division of labour and technocracy. Student ideology
attacked the ivory tower (or monastic) concept of a university and rejected
specific roles in favour of a charismatic personalism. I defended the
monasteries against the forces of dissolution.*

For many years after the technocrats built the Great City the
monks and the technocrats lived in peace. Indeed the monks hardly
ever came into the City (except to visit their wine merchants) and
preferred to live quietly in their stately houses. These were in
green pleasant places, often close by the banks of a stream.

Almost everybody felt kindly towards the good old monks.
They were occasionally quaint and precise about somewhat minor
matters but otherwise did no man any harm. In any case they
were greatly admired for their ability as cultivators. Their level of
cultivation was very high. It was widely held that three years spent
in the monasteries provided an excellent breathing time before the
real business of life should begin. Young people would lie by the
streams, join in the rites, speak about spiritual things with the
monks, and every now and then engage in a little cultivation.

The monks were careful scholars and in accordance with an
ancient vow of intellectual chastity bent all their energy to make
their studies pure. In the study of numbers, for example, they
achieved extraordinary heights of purity. Anything which was
'applied' smacked of the Great City and contravened the ancient

vow. All the same many were still not content with the standards of purity and entered more ascetic orders devoted to pursuits which were not only useless but which could obviously be recognized as such.

Meanwhile, in the Great City there was a great need for knowledge and many people prepared and ready to seek it. The technocrats believed that knowledge was to be sought after in monasteries and asked the good monks to build new foundations, to allow into their midst many youths who had spent all their lives in the Great City. These had maybe never even seen the long black robe of a monk, much less witnessed a performance of the ancient rites. Nevertheless, such youths prepared themselves by continuous spiritual exercises rising gradually from levels to degrees, happy in the promise that when they had spent their time with the monks they would become great men in the City. As for the monks they were full of sad foreboding, but they began to raise the new foundations, just as the technocrats had commanded them.

So the young men and women from the Great City sat at the feet of the monks and learnt many things, but most of all they learnt how to live in a monastery. Many indeed so loved the cloistered calm of their mentors that they wished never to leave it. Others stayed awhile and on their return to the Great City set up lay brotherhoods to cultivate themselves, just as did the good old monks. Yet others returned to the world only to find that the technocrats had deceived them and that they were not to be great men in the City but minor officials in distant provinces. And the more it became noised abroad that the technocrats were deceivers in this important matter, the more youths there were who wished never to leave the life of the cloister.

So the monasteries became full to overflowing, the ancient rites were disrupted and in many places ceased almost to be practised. The monks were blamed for serving the technocrats who had so deceived them; the technocrats were blamed for disturbing the hallowed ways of the ancient rule.

So it was that when the technocrats heard of all these things they began to build new houses, no longer in secluded valleys but in the

Great City itself. In these houses appeared orders of friars[1] whose business it was to think on the ways of the Great City and on the ancient knowledge of the monks, so that both should be brought together in harmony. They took no vows of purity and so were feared and despised by the monks. Because most of them lived in the City many were not experts in cultivation. On this account they could not be allowed in the more magnificent of the old monasteries. Instead, they brooded on the Great City, on the foolish cultivation of the monks and on the deceptions of the technocrats. And the youths who came to them brooded likewise.

Many were the things the friars preached about in the Great City, but the technocrats did not hear them. So the time came when the youths who sat listening in the great preaching houses said to the friars: to preach is not enough, more is required of you. No one here has taken the ancient vows and it is now time to turn knowledge into activity. How can he who has never himself acted truly know?

The friars themselves were divided. There were those who respected cultivation and did not hate the ancient vow even though they had never taken it themselves. Others left the preaching houses in anger and proclaimed the dawn of a new time as spoken of in the work of the old Abbott Herbert Marcuse:[2] when the monasteries should be dissolved, the Great City destroyed and all belong to the brotherhood. Such men gave themselves over to wild courses, singing bawdy songs, writing in a most scurrilous fashion and rushing about like so many sturdy beggars from place to place.

Seeing that vagrants did so greatly increase, and that the friars could barely control the perversity of the multitude the technocrats thought how they might bring all these things to an end. A few sturdy beggars were held in surety, but at this their fury only increased. Friars who had spent early years in the monasteries were charged with the oversight of the preaching houses, but to no effect. New houses were established where nothing was to be

[1] Social scientists.

[2] Spokesman of the Joachimite heresy. Actually, of course, Marcuse's message is not very hopeful.

taught but how youths should prepare themselves for the life of a minor official in the provinces. And the technocrats spoke with the friars how they might mend their preaching, no longer ranging in wild debate and heady talk, but attending only to one matter at a time and most soberly ascertaining the facts. Some were even cajoled into imitating the technocrats by converting seminars into laboratories and exchanging black robes for white coats. All was to no avail, and the vagrants only became the more tumultuous . . .

The end of the monks

Monachatus non est pietas. Monkishness is not true piety. This was the Protestant principle and it is also the policy of protesters in the contemporary university. The monastic insistence on contemplation and the academic commitment to objectivity are analogous, both in the nature of their aim and in the claim to a specialized, detached role. In the case of the academic his role requires a respect for criteria of objective validity, a careful sifting of evidence, and a disinterested stance *vis-à-vis* the world of man and nature. Such a stance does not require a disavowal of responsibility towards the world, especially perhaps towards the world of man, but it does mean that with regard to his own subject the academic should try to be neither the paid spokesman of an agency such as the state, nor the ideological representative of a cause.

Contemplation, discipline and objectivity are all under attack. To the extent that they reflect the tradition of 'remote and ineffectual' dons the attack has some justification. Academics belong to an open not a closed order, they are open brethren not exclusives. Moreover, no one doubts the loudest claims to objectivity often conceal the most subtle corrosions of bias. All the various intrusions of subjectivity have been recently much advertised. Yet this seems no reason to positively praise distortion in the interests of commitment or for letting the social imagination run riot simply because it is creative, dynamic and forward looking. These forms of radical subjectivity may correct an imbalance, but are in themselves quite opposed to the notion of a balance. Just as *sola fide* – faith alone – struck at the heart of monastic disciplines, so radical subjectivity strikes at the heart of academic disciplines. Intellectual antinomianism leads to an anarchy where there is no agreed basis of discussion and only the confrontation of viewpoints.

Universities, like monasteries, become corrupt, and fine ideals are used to cover the more insidious corruptions. Nobody need be surprised at that, except those who have no adequate measure of corruption in general. Monasteries and universities need reformation and reform, since they can all too easily remove the fuse from explosive ideas, become inextricably linked to a particular system of ownership, reflect a very partial viewpoint, drift into total irrelevance and so on. Yet without the monastic principle of partial detachment from society there would be little possibility of that catholic fusion of disparate disciplines with overall critical perspectives. Without monasticism, however deformed by a rigid demarcation of subjects, there is no 'universitas', no catholicity, but only expertise of varying kinds in polytechnics. Monasticism and vital criticism paradoxically require each other. Without monks no catholicity; and where catholicity is absent the end of the monks is near. Vocation becomes vocational. Or as Weber put it, the 'call' becomes the calling – the job. Men have to be very careful how they move towards the world because it generally has more power to absorb than they to reform.

The paradox can be illustrated by one young sociologist who said he had no intention of becoming a junior manager. As with so much current protest it is never quite clear whether the objection is to being a junior or being a manager, or indeed to the fact that nowadays a university education does not automatically lead to élite positions. Nevertheless, he had a fundamental objection to being incarcerated in a restrictive secular role with no 'spiritual' returns consonant with his horizons. Of course he also objected to the monastic concept of the university. Yet without the catholic perspectives of a university, and the ecumenical sweep of sociology, he could never have found the language of protest. Without that language he would have been a delinquent not a reformer.

Most reformers are like Martin Luther: ex-monks. They strive not only to reform but to destroy institutions without which they could not have come into existence. It is true that just as Protestants universalized monasticism by taking it into the world, so the protesters wish to universalize the university. The 'free university' is the monastery in the world, rebuilding that world under its immediate impact and responding to its most pressing problems. This is secularization. It is also the quickest way to be absorbed by the world, because once the vital energies of the moment are sapped and euphoria converted into boredom then the institutional framework of monastic life is needed, and not only institutionalization but discipline. Discipline is necessary and so are disciplines. The virtue of the old rule is discovery only when it is nearly lost.

No one denies that most universities exist in a social vacuum. The social seclusion of universities parallels the geographical seclusion of the monasteries. Indeed we still build universities in cathedral towns as if we have some feeling for their deep affinity. Curiously enough, it is this interstitial character which enables the prophet of revolt, Herbert Marcuse, to allot students a special role as the bearers of contemporary dynamism. The point is that they are not overwhelmed by secular cares and workaday restrictions of perspective. This enables them to think and act with wild abandon. So is is all very well for the reformers to repudiate the monastic principle by suggesting that opportunity for thought is useless without action, indeed that thought not based on action is itself emasculated. Without the monastic principle they would hardly have occasion for thought. The unity of theory and practice is the sort of half-truth always seized upon by reforming heretics and admittedly made the more persuasive when an ideal of the objectivity of thought is converted into an acceptance of a static 'objectivity' in the world, indeed into a world of 'objects'.[3]

So there is another parallel truth running in exactly the opposite direction which accuses the activist of using the social seclusion of the university as a false base for moral posturing and for emotional

[3] One should note in passing that the notion of the objectivity of truth is parallel to the concept of the transcendence of God. At every point current theological arguments find their analogies in the ideological dispute over the university.

dishonesty in defiance of objective, practical limitations. Even activist students are still contemplatives so long as they are at university: and some of them show remarkably little desire to leave its protective cloisters for the world. The conservative criticism has a justification. Students have no experience of life or of the precarious basis of such civilization as we have. They are supported in conceptual luxury by a wider society which they then abuse in total defiance of all conceivable likelihoods. Students moralize freely because they moralize at other people's expense, in both senses of the word expense. And it is even odder that the most chronic moralizers should be sociologists, because their sense of outrage can only be based on an incapacity to understand any sociology. This is why they turn sociology into ideology and justify themselves by claiming there is no difference.[4]

Not everybody can become an academic any more than the whole of life can become a seminar. Both the commercial right and the moralizing left are against the seminar mentality. Yet there must be people who accept the life of the cloister as their specialized vocation, if only because the politics of witness ought to depend on people who know the difference between true and false witness. 'Thou shalt not bear false witness' is one of the rules of monasteries and universities alike; it is as fundamental as the call not to be conformed to the world. Monks do not want everybody to have a vocation, but they do claim a right to a special vocation themselves. A civilization is lost when it dissolves its monasteries because the chief end of a monk is patient humility before the truth.

Ritual and the priesthood of all believers

The Protestant Reformers stood by the priesthood of all believers. Modern protesters stand by the participation of all students. The Reformers overthrew the Fathers; students overthrow their own

---

[4] Part of the trouble stems from the fact that sociology is the documentation of original sin by those who believe in original virtue.

fathers, and indeed, paternalism in general. Many of the Reformers were against ritual and so are many of the protesters, because ritual is an organized pattern of roles: father and son, priest and layman, teacher and student.

According to one student leader, teachers should merely be available to meet the collective requests of students when approached. The theory of the anti-university is that everybody 'says his bit and passes on'. This suggests that we may need no continuing university at all,[5] but rather a communal meeting-place where casual thoughts and maybe casual insults can be exchanged, roughly on the principle of the T group ... The result is the institutionalization of impertinence in every sense of the word. It is incidentally interesting that when *teachers* behave in this *ad hoc*, spontaneous way the demand is for *planned* seminars and for *office* hours, i.e. *more* bureaucracy.

The attempt to achieve a chaotic, revolving role structure applies even to the roles of leader and led. No 'leaders' must be allowed to emerge since leadership is a socially conferred role: the preferred mode is an alternating pecking-order of charismatic potency. And by a parallel development the abolition of horizontal lines between teacher and student requires the abolition of vertical lines between one subject and another.[6] The role of expert disappears, partly because expertise leads to mystification and so to power. Thus not only is bureaucracy rejected but also the division of labour: Weber *and* Durkheim. The shattered frame of the social cosmos is restored to the dynamic unity of a total *Gemeinschaft*. Marx *and* Tönnies.

Yet clearly not everybody belongs to this total *Gemeinschaft*. The true social cosmos (Luther's 'invisible church') consists of those whose eyes have been opened. It has no membership because that would confer a constricting identity. Hence, when I asked a girl if she belonged to the R.S.A. I found myself having to reformulate the question in terms of whether or not she was in the R.S.A. ambience! Even this degree of identification is plainly seen as near contamination. Radical students fear all categorization, by

[5] This is what radical theologians want to do to the Church.
[6] Not something incidentally to which I oppose blanket objections.

society or by sociologists.[7] By the same token there is no agreed dogma, even though there is plenty of dogmatism. Like some of the early Protestants there is a tendency to dissolve doctrine in psychology. One makes up doctrine as one goes along. This has the dual advantage of enabling very different and even opposed groups to work together and of avoiding criticism of the programme. Both doctrine and identity are given a hidden character, an adolescent inwardness, a youthful fluidity, preserving them from the adult intelligence and from middle-aged amusement. Like most people students fear hatred less than they fear laughter.

The priesthood of all believers is best symbolized in an established right to use a shortened version of anybody's Christian name at first acquaintance. Surnames belong to one's old secular persona: shortened Christian names belong to the brotherhood – Mike, Hank, Dave, Brett or whatever it may be. This is formalized in another established right to intrude fundamental dialogue without notice – as a man might look over the breakfast table and say 'Are you saved?' The point is that privacy, like tolerance, is seen as neglect, perhaps indifference, even contempt. So privacy is near-Fascist and even tiredness and sleep are reprehensible because they are closely related to apathy. Basic decencies associated with convention and social distance, are disregarded, whether or not they are based on status. Everyone has the right to treat anyone else as his brother whether his brotherly attentions are wanted or not. Intrusion becomes an art. The first sign of apathy, tolerance or indifference must be countered by a 'provocation' or a 'happening': these are the only true sacraments of revolutionary activism.

The major sacrament of counter-revolutionary apathy is a sherry party. The waters of Jerez are the gateway to Lethal forgetfulness, leading to compliance, convention, indifference, politeness, sensitivity, privacy. Good girl protesters have been known to declare that lips which touch sherry shall never touch theirs. It induces phantom consciousness. Academics who use it become ghosts in the machine – the machine of their role and of the bureaucracy. It helps them to fiddle while Vietnam burns. It is the class drink, the poisoned chalice. Oxbridge people are 'unreal'

[7] Teacher: 'Are you a second-year student?' Student: 'Don't objectify me.'

because they are known to drink it. N.U.S. diplomacy is stigmatized as 'sherry diplomacy' because it is unreal. The biggest insult
when radicals occupied a Senior Common Room at one university
was to be politely offered sherry.

All this is linked with an ancient malady to which students are
becoming increasingly prone: hypertrophy of the ontological
itch. No wonder there is a fringe of drug-taking. Certain social
types are stigmatized as ontologically deprived. Though students
claim every other deprivation, often on very slender grounds
indeed, at least they do not suffer the ultimate deprivations of
unreality. Indeed, they ask for more reality than is currently available. The deprived are the suburbanites who mow their lawns on
Sunday, are disciplined in their work, dress carefully, enunciate
clearly, marry institutionally and have two children. Real people
do not speak, but ejaculate elementally. Their marriages are un-
documented and they have no lawns to mow.

Sin

Protestantism and protest are concerned with sin: personal, or
universal, or specifically white European bourgeois sin. The saved
are those who have been made aware of sin, redeemed from false
consciousness. Sometimes protesters sit and collectively beat their
breasts for bourgeois decadence; it is not clear what it has to do
with them, but they evidently enjoy the penitential mood. They
are not so much concerned with the specific local sins of capitalist
society as with its structural sinfulness. This is in tune with the best
Protestant theology, except that the Protestant reference is
universal.

It also explains their attitude to violence. Capitalist civilization
is, in their view, endemically violent and the object of protest is to
unleash this institutional violence into public view. Similarly,
capitalist society is manipulative and so-called 'police brutality'
converts the psychological manipulation into physical manipulation: darkness visible. Because bourgeois society plans sin, it is – at
least according to one revolutionary sect – wrong to plan the acts

which bring it into the open. True provocation must arise spontaneously. This gives delinquency a theoretical justification: merely to throw a pebble at a hotel is malicious damage, but to throw it at the bourgeois mentality inside is an act of spontaneous moral revulsion. Ideological delinquency represents 'situation ethics' with a vengeance,[8] or if you like 'situation sin'; and it leads not to penitence but to the penitentiary.

When sin is structural, either in Adam or in the social system, any 'piecemeal social engineering' is by definition and by vocabulary merely manipulative. It tinkers with what properly deserves destruction. Even acts of charity become improper. A gift to a Vietnam orphanage can be described as a sop to conscience, almost indeed worse than useless, because it can enable the donor to live less harassed in the system as it is. Good works avail you nothing. Rather, the person whose eyes have been opened must feel free to act in *any* way against the structure, indeed against *structure as such*. *Pecca fortiter*. Luther or Genet.

The way out is through the 'dialectics of liberation', currently transferred to twenty-three gramophone records. In the Old Theatre at L.S.E. this was represented by a play concerned with the achievement of freedom. It began with silence and incense, and then became a morality play in reverse. (Catholicism produces morality plays; radical Protestantism plays against morality.) The message was very simple. We must try every possible combination of relationship and all will remain pure, provided they are not institutionalized: not the dialectics so much as the amateur dramatics of liberation.

This freedom is contrasted with academic freedoms; just as structural immorality is contrasted with piecemeal social engineering. Academics imagine they possess certain limited, institutionalized freedoms, but they are compassed about by a system which renders all of them null and void. They think they are free when – as Luther said – 'freewill is dead'. The teacher lives on a false consciousness from which he requires liberation. In their separated Senior Common Rooms they talk of insurances and mortgages.

---

[8] Another notion shared with the radical theologians: the absence of general moral rules complements the absence of institutions.

Students must liberate them from such divisive contexts and all concern with the morrow, if need be by 'occupation'. Those academics who see the student evangelists as mere diseased enthusiasts must remember that they desire nothing worse, or less, than their salvation.

The end of man

The use of theological language in the foregoing analysis is not merely a matter of useful analogy or suggestive comparison. To read Marcuse is reminiscent of reading dialectical theology. The ideas of Sartre on the maintenance of revolutionary *élan* are the problems already faced in the sociology of religion in the development of sectarian consciousness, especially routinization of charisma and the bureaucratization of the spirit. Moreover, the radicals in the Church run parallel to, and often overlap, the radicals in the university. In Germany the religious elements and personnel in the protest have been remarked upon; and there has been a striking absence of the irreligion traditionally current among rebels. This is partly because the radicals in the Church draw on the same phenomenological, existentialist, humanizing, personalist – and ultimately Protestant and Hebraic traditions, as do many radicals in the university. Indeed there is something very proper in the fact that so many of our modern Protestants are Hebrews.

So the crisis runs back to the roots of our civilization: to its vital Hebraic component and to those two institutions which have a special social charter in terms of the injunction to be in the world and not of it. Because Church and university have this intrinsic spiritual element written into their charters they evoke the strongest loyalties and the most vigorous repudiations: loyalty to their aspiration, repudiation of their failures. The middle position between unthinking loyalty and unrealistic repudiation is the monastic and academic tradition, which tries to achieve the highest aspirations in limited enclave. But this too invites its own corruptions, and creates a demand that the order leave the cloister and march into the world. The social élite must be evicted from the monasteries and the spiritual élite must leaven the lump of the secular world by itself becoming secularized.

Yet the Church and the university not only have spiritual aims but unite them with the task of moral and intellectual socialization. Originally this was done in close partnership until the differentiation of modern society split the roles between them: the university now has little to do with morals, and to the extent that the Church still has a continuing task of moral socialization, this has little to do with intellectual training. Yet, for various historical reasons the Church remains identified as a socializing agency when in fact it is being reduced perilously close to its fundamental *raison d'être*: the realm of the spirit. This is both dangerous and fruitful since all the lesions, disjunctions and backlogs of sudden social change have resulted in the tensions of the spirit becoming partly disembodied from their traditional language and institutional location. Hence the Church only partially reflects these tensions, just as it only partially performs the role of socialization.

The spirit attempts to relocate itself in the university. It cannot be disembodied, but there is an immediate problem of the right relation between spiritual aspects and other social functions. Just as the spirit cannot be disembodied, so no institution can exist *only* to express the spirit, because the spiritual and the secular are woven together not only empirically but also theoretically in the texture of western civilization. For the Church the problem was how to articulate a right relation between moral socialization and the spiritual dynamism of the Gospel. For the university now it is an even more complex task of articulating the right relation between economic and technical imperatives, intellectual socialization, and the urge to moral and spiritual activism.

When the Church was almost entirely bound up with moral socialization Protestantism attempted to break through the system by repudiating the whole structure of moral levels, and disciplines as mere works of the flesh. In the same way contemporary protesters try to wreck the whole system of levels, and degrees, of packaging and processing currently involved in intellectual socialization. Where the Protestants substituted the category of saved and unsaved the protesters substitute the category of true and false consciousness.

Yet the distinction between true and false consciousness, though related to, is *not* identical with, the distinction between truth and falsehood. It is this confusion which results in spiritual hubris, intellectual antinomianism and indiscipline of every kind. A vital relationship is converted into a near identity: learning is not therapy, knowledge is not ideology, because contemplation and action are neither identities nor rivals but complementary.

In a way, of course, all this has to do with the great Weberian themes and we must recognize the valid elements in the current protest. It attempts to counteract acquiescence, consensus politics, the divisive character of multiplying roles, anonymity, the elongated structure of bureaucratic power, indeed the whole process of rationalization conceived apart from overriding human purpose. It rejects knowledge without understanding, processes without community, power without purpose.

Weber argued that an indirect mutation of the Protestant spirit was essential to the birth of the modern world of capitalism and bureaucracy. By a curious irony it is an indirect mutation of capitalism and bureaucracy which produces the protesting spirit, not now canalized and distorted either by the psychic disciplines of capitalist accumulation or by the work disciplines of industrialism, but in a world of increasing automation and leisure able again to ask its own proper question: 'What is the chief end of Man?'[9]

[9] Scottish Shorter Catechism.

4.   The Nursery of Revolution

This essay was a response to the central phase of the conflict in which the radical students attempted occasional occupations and variously put forward notions of the university as a 'red base' or as the ideal centre for therapeutic anarchy. By this time relations between academics were deeply strained. Some, like myself, were organizing themselves to bolster up administrative resistance; others concluded that however unfortunate student behaviour might be there could be no enemies on the left when it came to a confrontation with the establishment. At the same time the perfervid psychology of student radicals was becoming the object of some curiosity. The reversion to childishness and addiction to paranoid fantasy stimulated many observers to speculate on the origins of these phenomena in misunderstandings of Freudian theory.

Ever since Imagination seized Power in England's premier school of the social sciences the overheated air of that institution has been thick with immodest proposals for the abolition of this and the total transformation of that. One of the most intriguing has been the suggestion that the London School of Economics be converted into the Croydon Finishing School for Young Socialists. Another pleasing possibility put about by a student newsheet is that the college should be re-created as the London School of Untram-melled Desire. According to this proposal the motto 'Rerum cognoscere causas' should be immediately replaced by 'The Only Law is – "Do what thou wilt".'[1] But the most interesting of all the plans for a yet more glorious future has been the setting up of a Houghton Street Day Nursery of Revolution.[2] Here indeed is a

[1] 'Beaver', 24 October 1968.
[2] Houghton St.: the narrow defile in which stands the main entrance of the L.S.E.

37

TRACTS AGAINST THE TIMES

new and exciting concept of the modern role of a university and one to which we have already made so much progress that little more may be required than a simple change of name. Since the concept is so potent and the realization so nearly achieved one or two comments and queries are hardly out of order.

One of the consequences of this recent development has been, for good or ill, that academics now barely experience any awareness of a change when they pass from home to work or from week to weekend. Previously a weekend with the children was very different from a week at the School. At home the children were fascinating creatures, exposed to every irrational whim, quite amoral and charmingly spontaneous. One moment they would bury their heads in your bosom, the next beat you unmercifully between the eyes. Students on the other hand appeared as responsible adults, apparently well able to look after themselves without detailed supervision, and content with reasonable fulfilments of academic duty. At home the children wanted to be loved; at university the students wanted to be taught. The transition from one to the other seemed clear.

Then quite suddenly all was changed. The façade of disciplined student endeavour was rolled away revealing an entirely new scenario in the making: the Houghton Street Day Nursery of Revolution. The young adults disappeared into the wings and in their place there entered a new set of fascinating creatures, quite amoral and alarmingly spontaneous, demanding at one moment to bury their heads in your bosom and the next beating you unmercifully between the eyes. The very revelation of this new scenario tore off the scales from the vision of the academics and achieved one major objective of the revolution: the abolition of the difference between home and work, labour and leisure. The life of the academic became all of a piece: he just moved from one nursery to another.

Academics are, by habit, disinclined to believe their eyes, but a whole series of changes confirmed this original impression. The first was a bare-faced disregard for truth on the part of his charges. Whereas the adult student had always been slightly shamefaced about fabrication the denizens of the Day Nursery of Revolution positively celebrated it. They claimed that the invention of truth was better than reality – as indeed it was.[3] In their view the great defect of bourgeois science was that it could not make the truth up as it went along. The older type of student had only done this under pressure in examinations: he had hardly thought of making it *the* principle of scientific activity. It had not occurred to him that he was actually superior to the sordid requirements of mere objectivity and the heavy chains of bourgeois logic. But in the Nursery such things only weighed down the achievements of the imagination. The child constructs his own world. Anyone who contradicts that world he treats with a knowing grin of superior ignorance.

Apart from the new found power of fantasy the Day Nursery revealed an incipient thuggishness. It appeared that occupation was nine-tenths of the law. Wants and demands varied violently from one moment to the next. Egocentric autonomy co-existed with instant recourse to the maternal breast. Academics were required to be immediately available but not to interfere. The Nursery was *their* territory: there was no notion of neutral space. All the toys and apparatus belonged to the children by absolute right and they might use them if and when they wanted: the adult world owed them not merely a living but a leisured existence. All adult rules were resented but no one doubted the adults would appear with the goodies when the proper time for them came around.

The main activity of the Nursery of Revolution was drama. In the darkest corner of the Nursery is to be found an Old Theatre,[4] so called because the same childish scenes are re-enacted there year after year. There the children use their imaginations and play at revolution. They never tire of these endless scenes and enormously prefer them to contact with the outside world. This pleasure in make-belief explains phrases like 'Storm the Reality Studio' and 'Retake the Universe'.

Now that the principle and practice of the Nursery is so well established the L.S.E. academics naturally vary in their reaction: some for example are very reactionary indeed. Other academics

[3] The invention of truth is *their* phrase.
[4] The Old Theatre where most of the student revivals occur.

have been so sheltered from reality by longish sojourn in the university that the Theatre of the Absurd does not strike them as in the least peculiar. This type of academic has the kind of centre which always has a soft spot for the wet left.

Yet other academics desperately wish to join again in the great dramas of youth. Some very curious symptoms follow as a result. For example they suffer acute confusion between paedogogy and paedophilia. To take another example they become unable to distinguish being lit-up from being enlightened. To join in the spontaneous life of the Nursery seems to provide the best guarantee against crabbed age and dull responsibility. They even develop a positive preference for ignorance and immaturity.

In a sense some academics discover in the Nursery a new version of *in loco parentis*. Nevertheless the role of the parent who indulgently eggs the children on to new forms of high-spirited and lovable mischief is not an easy one. He is only really wanted when there is some danger the mischief will annoy the neighbours to the point where they will do something about it. Apart from this the 'old boy' is dispensable. In any case the new version of *in loco parentis* is not really just what the old academic might wish. The real desire is less for an indulgent parent than a kind of private tutor: the sort of hapless scholarly attendant who waits upon the impetuous whim of the young master. This may suggest a new interpretation of the famous remark 'We must educate our masters'. The Nursery is indeed gradually moving towards this particular revolutionary notion of the academic role: one student actually complained to me that after having got excited about a book in the library he was unable to discuss it with his tutor for a *whole week*.

The capacity of the Houghton Street Day Nursery of Revolution to create a reaction has already been referred to. Those who 'react' are known as 'reactionaries' and are the embodiment of Incarnate Evil. They may be politically well to the left but a reactionary is currently defined as one who thinks 'we are none of us infallible, not even the youngest of us'. These people form the demonology of the Nursery. Ordinary nurseries are peopled by fairies, hobbits, elves, hobgoblins, trolls and so on. Students don't believe in fairies but they believe the evidence for demons is cumulative and irrefutable. Their world is peopled by monstrous creatures, such as governors, professors, politicians, bureaucrats, capitalists, journalists and so on, about whom they constantly claim to be 'frightened', whose activities they refer to as 'sinister'. These creatures are believed to be about to hand them all over to be eaten by ogres in the Stock Exchange. All events in the outside world are explained in a few key formulae about the machinations of the demonic capitalists and bureaucrats: this childish gabble is most easily picked up by the bright as well as most quickly dropped by them. Such explanations are basically not much superior to my son's explanation of why he gets up in the night, 'pink elephants are biting me'. Unfortunately his formulae and theirs both take a considerable time to refute. On the other hand they also believe the brutal bureaucratic trolls can be spirited out of existence by a single stroke of the imagination: as one student stated 'We have made the ruling classes tremble'. No wonder they claim imagination has seized power: not only has it seized power it has – literally – run riot.

Commentary on the nursery story

How do we explain the re-appearance of the Nursery? Is infantile regression really a revolutionary threat? These questions prompt two further questions. The first concerns the way in which we treat people in the genuine nurseries at home and also in the schools, the nurseries of future citizens. The second is whether our civilization is so secure that widespread indulgence in the fantasies of childhood – maybe throughout a lifetime – is something it can withstand without breakdown.

In our society we have gained the kind of control over external necessities which can enable large sections of the community, especially of course students, to maintain flights from reality over considerable periods of time. Not many of us are like the Police or the Army actually engaged on tasks at the frontiers of society where failure has serious consequences. To engage on collective tasks where there is risk provides a sharp check on fantasy. But as Professor MacRae has pointed out students experience a world in which the machines have never stopped and show no sign of stopping. So they can be the flower children who gaily crowd on the social band wagon. Like the aesthetes of the 90s they *are* the civilization the rest of us are working for. So it is not surprising they insist on a specious identification with the working class because it is the workers – of whatever class – who make their luxurious and disordered imaginations possible. This basic contradiction – to use their terminology – is responsible for yoking the psychology of the aesthetic to the philosophy of Marxism. So it is perhaps some inkling of their own impotent theatricality which makes them pose as the dynamic element in society. This is particularly true for the sociologists: what the practical is for the physical scientist the 'demo' is for them.

This increased possibility of persistent infantilism is connected with the fact that a misreading of Freud has made us such timid parents that our children are under-socialized, inadequately prepared for social realities. We are so afraid of making them conformists and so guilty about making them guilty that the process of socialization has been inverted. The twentieth century has stood Freud on his head. It is the socializing *agents* – parents and teachers – who feel guilt.

Now there is a partial gain here: for previous generations education and upbringing was a form of over-kill. All 'contrary imaginations' were crushed in order to prepare the young victims for a narrowing, limiting reality. Life was conceived as a relentless March, an inevitable Task. Now, however, the Task-Force has disappeared, the symbolic drill has dissolved into physical expression, and the March has become a Ramble.[5] The structure of grammar has disintegrated into creative writing. The gain is more than the loss, but the loss is considerable, since not *all* of life can be a Ramble, and for those whose education suggests that it is the

[5] The half-way house is the Boy Scout Movement, quite explicitly a target for radical vituperation. In the Boy-Scouts it is surrogate fathers who *organize* rambles and cover their activities by adopting symbolic disguises and fictitious identities.

reality, principle can be staved off for a very long time. Moreover, life at a university requires the kind of self-discipline for which neither marches nor rambles are adequate preparation. So much educational rambling is in any case partly an excuse for intellectual laziness and pedagogical sloppiness. Of course many of our grammar schools are still run like task-forces of the old-fashioned type but there is enough of the other mode in the educational system to inculcate contrary imaginations and even to exacerbate them by inconsistencies between different stages of the process.

When we define youth as automatically innocent and creative it obviously is difficult to make the transition from youth to adulthood and responsibility. Who would want to exchange automatic innocence for automatic guilt, the right to blame freely for the right to be freely blamed? At the same time some minimal responsibility is almost unavoidable and the first initiation into adulthood is often the arrival of children. When this happens the undersocialized parent is himself too frightened to socialize: the most he can accept is the role of elder brother, which enables him to retain the illusion that he is still not saddled with ultimate responsibility for what happens. The result is the appearance of children who both demand to have real parents and who detest parents. And just as the initiation into responsibility of parenthood causes a trauma of withdrawal so does the initiation into concrete social responsibilities. Thus the academic, faced with a position of responsibility fears that he is at heart no longer a student, no longer the eager-eyed vanguard of the future. So he too steps aside and takes the role of the totally indulgent parent, seeing in each childish folly a new revelation of innocent creativity.

All these themes come to a focus in relation to the necessary forces of order in society and the psychology which must lie behind such forces – in any society. This psychology was common to all of us when social roles were less minutely sub-divided, when external necessity pressed more heavily on us – in short when for the vast majority of people life could not be conceived other than as a Task. Now however, very different psychologies can coexist in society and the free-floating imagination of the student can coexist with the psychology of the task and – among the forces of order – the psychology of authority and obedience. In short the mentality of the police *in any society* is a vicarious sacrifice for the mentality of indulgent creativity. And in our society we can actually afford more of the indulged creators. Nevertheless the possibility of the under-socialized student depends on the certainty of the over-socialized policeman, not to mention the disciplined dedication of the teacher.[6]

It is precisely this symbiosis which can give rise to an extreme hatred between the two polar sections of society, and as usual such hatred is expressed in sexual terms. (One student pamphlet for example refers to the police as not merely 'the pigs' but as 'flat-footed, duck-arsed eunuchs.') The policeman is anal: all his functions are controlled. The student is pre-anal: his functions are spontaneous. By the same token the student is a symbol of disorderly innocence and the policeman a symbol of corrupt order. If the student kicks the policeman it arises from spontaneous revulsion; if the policeman kicks the student it is evidence of systematic brutality. Hence the student who throws excrement in the policeman's face really is asserting his pre-anal innocence.

One final point: I have argued that student anarchism depends on the discipline of those who work, his disorder on the certainty that others will patrol the streets and maintain the law for him. He attacks paternalism in the sure and certain hope that indulgent elders will continue to act *in loco parentis*. This symbiosis tells us something about student revolutionary potential. The antinomian heresy – 'Do what thou wilt' – has never spawned a lasting revolution. A mixture of student aestheticism and theatricality is a much greater nuisance than it is a danger. The social relationships of the Nursery may be boring and infuriating but hardly a challenge to the adult world. The older style of revolutionary disciplined himself and was cruelly anal in his irrevocable March towards a New Society. He was collectively his own police and army and a terrible job he made of it. But where he failed the political equivalent of a

---

[6] And it may be said that the supposed connection between creativity and disorder is generally overstated: the Puritans are also great creators just as they are usually the great revolutionaries.

children's nature ramble is hardly likely to succeed.[7] The whole enterprise depends too much on what it pretends to overthrow. Or to put it another way: anarchism and vitalism are excellent attitudes for social parasites but are not serious political philosophies. It is the Puritans who make revolutions, even in England. One need not worry too much about long-haired Cavaliers decked out in the trimmings of Carnaby Street.

[7] For the most consistent statement of radical anti-political instinctualism and indeed the main tendency of student attitudes one should consult the works of Wilhelm Reich. Rousseau is of course the fundamental source and – as I have argued elsewhere – the antinomian wing of the Reformation. cf. P. Rieff *The Triumph of the Therapeutic* (1966).

5. *The End of the Protestant Ethic*

The essay on this topic dates from a period of deepening bitterness which immediately preceded a period of astonishing calm. Student attacks on critical academics were scabrous, anonymous and libellous. Psychological intimidation was frequent and campaigns of malicious slander accepted as part of everyday life. To anyone brought up on Protestant (or Kantian) notions of devotion to work and concern for veracity and consistency this particular spectacle of adolescent rebellion was merely contemptible. The bitter tone of my comments on this phase derives from my experience as the person in charge of graduate studies in the department of sociology. It was also fed by their 'trial' of me for the offence of being on their premises. A small mob conducted this piece of third degree while others called the police in order to accuse me of having done so and to accelerate confusion and anger amongst students. When I succeeded in sending the police away the soi-disant students proceeded to break a large number of windows in the newly built sections of the School.

Perhaps the most important thing to say is that although the tendencies described here are drawn from the British experience, nevertheless British Universities are amongst the quietest in the world. The examples are drawn from the London School of Economics, but do not apply to a majority of students even there. What is true, however, is that a minority of a certain kind can still be immensely damaging to scholarly work and autonomy and that the majority have enough sympathy with the catchwords, enough affinities with their psychological set, enough ignorance of what is actually happening, and enough generational solidarity to side with them in clashes with authority. An attack on the extremists is easily felt to be an attack on students as such. No one acquainted with the pitched battles between thousands of rival left wing students in Japan, or with the 'trashing' activities which damaged all property within a half-mile radius of the University of Wisconsin, can consider the L.S.E. extremists as other than a quiet community of well-mannered scholars. Moreover they will probably unlearn their lunatic attitudes on entering the wider world – after all traditional students at Oxbridge have not necessarily always been examples of earnest endeavour – and behind the strained postures there do lurk pertinent questions. It is also important to realize that the psychology of disorder and 'creativity' here described is opposed by groups like the Trotskyists which actually represent a secularized and revolutionary version of the Protestant Ethic. Thus when the L.S.E. was taken over the place was *organized* and left unusually *clean*. Meanwhile those with anarchic inclinations virulently attacked what they called the 'hang ups' of 'the organizers.' Trotskyite journals even pride themselves on their followers being carefully shaved. So one must remember there is more than one minority in this situation; in fact there are about as many warring sects as there are organizations of Palestinian guerillas.

To begin. Not long ago in *The Listener* Richard Hoggart composed an obituary for the Protestant Ethic. Since it was in fact his own obituary there was a natural tinge of sadness, but on the whole he did not lament the passing of the stern imperatives of *guilt* and *work*. I suppose that three years or so ago I might have agreed with him, but when a certain critical proportion of people in your immediate environment have given up guilt and work, the disadvantages strike one more forcibly. If a given percentage of people give up working the rest have to work harder. Those who do not feel guilty will exploit others without even noticing it. That is irritating and annoying, especially when the exploiters regard themselves as the exploited and when they demand to be regularly and efficiently serviced by those whom they simultaneously despise for regularity of life and devotion to organization.

Intellectual Law and Personal Order

Perhaps most people round about forty are visited with a sense of generational lapse, but there are those of my generation who note precisely the same features of current psychology only to applaud it and vicariously to renew their youth. What I note personally is something like this. The present generation claims to exercise creativity and flexibility outside the restraints of structures. These structures include sequences of work, consistencies of plan and motivation, organized categories and distinctions. In short they have been reared and socialized in a way that destroys their capacity for intellectual law and personal order.

A generalization is an offence against individuality: it is first cousin to a *rule*. A category is a mere abstraction and a constriction of an undifferentiated reality. A social role is not the basis of an organized, located activity but a restriction of the person. A goal is not a challenge to achieve but an artificial limitation of horizon. Most older people are glad to have eyes only in the front of their head in order to focus purposefully on particular objects but this type of young person regards the ability to focus as a constriction and the fact that eyes are only on one side of the head as a way of ignoring the fact that the horizon consists of 360°. To quote one of their slogans 'we want it *all now*.'

Once people of this kind arrive at the University, they reject its intellectual disciplines in favour of personal expression and osmotic absorption. One student gave up attending seminars because (I quote) 'My ideas were distorted by the imposition of logic.'[1] However, because they cannot achieve a sustained focus or organize their activity over a time span, they have also to exhibit attitudes of exploitative dependence on teachers. They simultaneously demand total freedom of choice and are unable to work independently. Hence they vehemently reject all father figures and demand wet nurses, declare all men equal without distinction of knowledge, age or experience and then treat the old and the scholarly as a variety of servant class.

---

[1] This particular student was then offered a thesis topic instead of the highly flexible but structured course he had originally chosen. He announced his topic as 'A Study of the Way in Which the University inhibits creativity.'

Caprice of Student Representatives

Freedom in this chaotic, undifferentiated sense also implies caprice: just as the child veers in his wants and demands so too does the student. If one assumes his demands are rational and long-term, one is soon disabused by finding that once one demand is satisfied a more extreme and often contradictory one takes its place. Thus at one and the same meeting with students one may encounter an imperious demand that teachers 'implement without delay' a complete reorganization of the curriculum and teaching method *and* the assertion that teachers ignore the fact that students are naturally very ignorant and inexperienced so they cannot be reasonably expected to read long or difficult books. At the very next meeting another proposed reform of curriculum will appear which is quite contrary in its implications, and it may easily be asserted students are so well informed and up-to-date that professors are entirely unnecessary. One week students ask for a *carte-blanche* to run a seminar by free association, the next week they are complaining that teachers have made inadequate efforts to plan it on a long-term basis. And so on. This is reinforced wherever volatile students insist that delegates constantly report back to and reflect the 'consciousness' of the mass and require that delegates should be rapidly replaced to ensure they don't form rapport with teachers, or indeed acquire necessary information. After enough experiences of this kind, the teachers become irritated even with suggestions that might have some rational substance. Similarly, subjected to an adequate amount of contradictory abuse they become sensitively alert to the imperious contemptuous manner that frequently accompanies student 'demands.' These demands employ a bullying tone which would have done no discredit to the supervisor of a badly run plantation.

This rapidly veering psychology rooted in the undifferentiated world of the child – or the drug addict – and sometimes amusingly described by student ideologues as 'mounting revolutionary consciousness' is not mere petulance. It connects historically with the anarchic undercurrent of previous revolutionary movements, except that in this particular case the revolutionary potential is dissipated by the predominance of the anarchic tendency. However, the movements of the past, whether political or religious (such as the antinomian heresy) frequently not only embodied these intensely contradictory phenomena, such as the tension between orderly Puritanical discipline in the pursuit of revolutionary aims and infantile disintegration, but also went through sequences from the one to the other. In Germany the anarchist phase has already partly flowed back into the ideological and psychological rigidities of Marxism-Leninism. Even in the British situation one can discern a sequence from the slogan 'make love not war' to a glorification of violence as the key to reality. It is a very curious experience to watch sometime devotees of 'love' being conscientiously instructed in the techniques of injecting police horses, pulling police off their mounts, breaking police formations and inciting them to 'brutality' by sustained campaigns of contempt and insult. Moreover, whether the students concerned believe in making love or in making war they both tend to prefer the intimate, paranoid, and sometimes conspiratorial atmosphere of their sects or of their drop-out liaisons to the older type of 'Student Society.' Though there is a great deal of talk about 'isolation' the Student Society often dies of attrition while the conspiratorial group flourishes. It is the impact of these groups which caused one philosopher to complain that 'not one of them dares think a thought without permission of a crowd.'

Motives Are the Highest Possible

Of course to the commonsense of the outsider these activities appear as mere adolescent delinquency. What is special about student adolescents, however, is that they are intelligent enough to appear as delinquent wolves in ideological sheeps' clothing. They know how to be lazy as a matter of moral principle, and how to be delinquent for the highest possible motives. Such a combination of indulgent and vicious behaviour with superior moral insight can hardly fail to be uniquely seductive. It is just this assumption of free-wheeling moral superiority which uses the medieval idea of the university as an inviolable sanctuary to put the student above the operation of the law. Thus a section of L.S.E. students augmented (as usual) by a motley collection of outsiders staged a 'Festival of Oppression' within its sacred walls, apparently hoping to induce an act of oppression from the authorities. Since this was not forthcoming one group decided to 'create' it and to cause a panic by a bogus call to the police, while another small group conducted a 'trial' of me as Dean for the offence of being on *their* premises.

It is very difficult not to link this erosion of the Protestant Ethic and this psychology of the osmotic splurge with excesses associated with current educational theory. Such educational theory is strongly reinforced in the rearing practices of the 'progressive' middle class. Thus academics frequently note with rueful candor that the worst cases are often the children of academics brought up on potent misunderstandings of Freud. (Freud noted that civilization depended on repression: his followers often draw the conclusion 'so much the worse for civilization'.) This is not the place to describe this fashionable educational theorizing, but it frequently attempts to dissolve logic in creativity, sequence in disorganized flexibility, and testable capabilities in the intuiting of notions. It propagates itself by an esoteric and approved vocabulary which is often little more than concept dropping. It does not build character or impart skills or provide mere information:[2] all these are inferior aims to the eliciting of sensitivities. Such sensitivities never seem to require hard work nor is there any suggestion that desired objectives may need unpleasant and persistent grind. Life need be no more than the extension of happy consciousness.

I exaggerate, of course, to bring out a contrast, but the tendencies and the situation in the schools are real enough. Children whose life and learning have been disrupted in this way, and who can no more conceive of a grammatical rule than of a school regulation, are conspicuously unprepared for the intellectual disciplines of a university, let alone the social disciplines of the

---

[2] I am not a devotee of spelling but it is worth noting that this year I marked a university finals script in which 'his' and 'has' were spelt 'is' and 'as'.

world outside. But they need not worry about the disciplines of the world outside, partly because it is now very difficult to remove people from the university but also because the disciplines of survival have weakened even in the world of industry. British youth has already been removed from the disciplines of survival associated with national service or actual war and they do not anticipate too much struggle for survival even in industry. One does not need to approve either militaristic dragooning, or robot-like learning or cutthroat competition to notice how crazy the excesses can be in the opposite direction and how far the reality principle is ignored.

Reality Does Not Remove Work

Indeed it has been frequently commented that members of the British Labour Party and the Social Democratic Party, as well as old-fashioned Marxists, are strongest in their rejection of this educational disintegration. We are, after all, as Richard Lowenthal has pointed out, not *yet* in the post-industrial society. Skills and capabilities and professional competence still need to be acquired, graded and certificated by appropriate authorities. Conspicuous achievements need to be openly recognized. People even have to earn their living. The trouble is that there are not enough jobs around which are specially designed for creative personalities. Where a previous generation asked for work, this particular minority of the present generation asks for something wherewith to express itself. This is what they regard as 'real'. Indeed they feel 'unreal' *both* because they have been so sheltered from reality *and* because reality does not ultimately shelter them from the constraints of ordinary life and work. They suffer from what can only be called ontological deprivation, and violence is quite frequently praised as a key to the recovery of 'reality'. As the motto embroidered on a member of 'The Soft Machine' put it: *Explode Reality*.

All this contrasts with the 'Protestant Ethic' of independence, responsibility for the self, restraint, achievement, diligence and attention to fact and to the printed word. One could go through these elements of the Protestant Ethic one by one, but I can only select one or two of them.

Take attention to facts, whether facts about persons or scientific and historical facts: there is a notable indifference to both. Student newspapers are increasingly written by specialists in obscenity, mendacious rumour and anonymous libel. If this seems an exaggerated judgment, only the briefest survey of student productions will verify it in profuse detail. It is often extremists of precisely the kind I have described who somehow secure control of student newspapers (and of unsigned news-sheets), frequently in defiance of the student union to whom the newspaper nominally belongs. Thus the student body is subjected to a constant diet of vilification and misrepresentation directed against staff and administration for which the complicated law of libel (let alone tactical considerations) barely allows redress. Character-assassination is regular and accepted, especially of any teacher who stands up to student demands. To take another example, when the Director of L.S.E. challenged student representatives with the repetition of allegations that the school received tied money from industrial donors, a student replied that the *factual* truth or otherwise of such allegations was irrelevant. The important point for him was that such allegations served to indicate the school's metaphysical implication in the social system.

Take responsibility: everything which goes wrong is conveniently blamed onto the system. Again, extremely dubious notions derived from psychiatry and sociology assist in destroying the notion of personal responsibility. I once diverted myself by dropping the word 'duty' into a conversation as if I did not realize it was laughable, and was duly rewarded with amused smiles of incredulous contempt. The following quotation is an adequate illustration of what I mean because it accepts the factuality of these contentions only to blame them exclusively on the system and on the supposed oppressiveness of the most 'liberal' university in the United Kingdom:[3]

> There is a great deal of casual sex, casual theft, casual vandalism, casual squalor which I think is a product of the very oppressive

[3] Essex.

environment. There are a lot of people who don't like the university and they have to get back at it. So they set fire to the notice boards or steal anything movable.

If you are a socialist here you *just don't think of getting a job with a firm*. Maybe you think of teaching, or television, or postgraduate work. *But any kind of job becomes tainted*. A lot of people are very afraid about what will happen when they leave (quoted from *The Times*, August 1970; my italics).

The same applies to work. One young academic told me how much it had embarrassed him to describe a student in a reference to an employer as 'diligent'. I appeared to sympathize but suggested that there might easily be categories of employment where attention to work was regarded as positively advantageous. He replied that could only be matter of *cultural lag*. He meant that work was out-of-date.

Finally take attention to the *word*. In one sense the radical extremist is a specialist in words. The production of words in meetings of extremists is prodigious in quantity. In these meetings the facile rhetoric of liberty and participation is infinitely transferable without regard to context (unhappily, politicians anxious to be acceptable to the young frequently accede to this rhetoric just as do many administrators anxious not to have their institutions publicized by 'trouble'). And yet there is a mistrust of all structured, prepared speech, and of all kinds of expression which are precise, elegant, rhythmically balanced and carefully qualified. Often the approved mode of expression is a series of half-audible existential grunts. This is because structured speech is related to personal control and also because of an extreme philosophical relativism that believes nothing can truly be said which is not an appeal to personal authenticity. Mere verbal courtesy is thought to be treachery against the inner self. Indeed amongst the paradoxes of extremism is the contrast between intense dogmatism and a degree of refusal to accept anything which easily leads to total verbal withdrawal and a sort of drooping silence.

All the above could be illustrated by copious examples. It might be appropriate, however, to conclude by just one example which did not at all involve the kind of extremist described here. This example indicates the character of the wider problem and its intractability.

During the Autumn term I both increased the number of scheduled classes in response to student requests as well as maintaining a group of unscheduled classes. Few of those who asked for the increase in scheduled classes bothered to come to them and about four people only attended the unscheduled ones. At the first session of the Summer term no one attended even the normal scheduled class. I therefore put up a notice to say that I now had a fair notion as to how much intellectual thirst remained unslaked and that additional and unscheduled classes would be henceforth cancelled. A day or two later I greeted a member of the class in the street. He said 'What are you doing there, smiling and saying "hello" when you've cancelled our class?' I replied rather coolly that I was talking with a colleague and inquired why nobody had turned up. 'You can't expect *us* to turn up on only the second day of term' he said, 'we were ready to come *this* week. I call your behaviour staff delinquency. After all, aren't you paid to teach?' 'Amongst other things' I said, 'and not when there are no students.' I then rehearsed the history of student delinquency, including an early end to the previous term as well as a late beginning to the present one, and the story of the four interested students. 'Three or four is very nice and cosy' he said, 'I'd have come to those. The trouble with your classes is they're too big.' (They were ten to twelve.) 'Not last week they weren't' I repeated. And so on.

A minor irritation is illustrated in this example – but it points up the general discourtesy, a lack of genuine desire to implement requests which have been met and the waste of time so often involved in trying to meet them. It also points to the fact that so-called moderates and the silent majority are frequently as little interested in learning or in the virtues of the Protestant Ethic as an extremist for whom the very notion of a rational structure of any kind is anathema. Faced with both kinds of students it is no wonder that one famous German scholar recently wondered whether he was now fighting a losing battle against a major decline in western civilization.

6. Young Men Seeing Visions

This essay, printed in The Christian Century (*September 9, 1970*), *began as a sermon preached on Education Sunday of that year. I was concerned to contrast the 'Sheltered Generation' for whom welfare and work were relatively assured with the previous generation who had had to fight to achieve both. Welfare and work had required bureaucracy, yet the radical young rejected these preconditions of administrative socialism. Instead they concentrated on the salvation of their own souls, but without any concept of the cost of such redemption. They were unlike old style socialists in that they rejected the administrative apparatus of welfare socialism (and the tyrannical apparatus of Soviet socialism) and unlike old-style Christians in that redemption came quite naturally.*

When I define the older generation in Great Britain as one made up of persons over 23 I realize that I exaggerate. In any case, the older generation is defined not by age but by experience: what it was like to be shaped by the years between 1929 and 1950 – between the beginning of the great economic slump and the end of wartime austerity. The younger generation is shaped by relative plenty and by no immediate contact with the realities of war. In that they are the Sheltered Generation: sheltered as no generation has ever been not only in British history but in the history of humanity.

This is the central and startling fact: those British young people brought up in the conditions created by the Attlee government and under the protecting shadow of the United States have had a new experience, whereby a sufficient number of things have altered in their environment to make a *qualitative* difference in that experience as a whole. True, privileged groups enjoyed similar securities before them, and underprivileged groups remain in our society who only partially possess them now. But vast numbers have crossed the crucial divide.

When Death Was Ever with One

Consider with me for a moment the earlier experience – that of the '20s, '30s and '40s. People then lived in a world governed by necessity and necessities. Let me exaggerate again to bring out a contrast: that older world was governed by the necessity of work and the necessity of death.

What do I mean by the necessity of death? I used the word 'exaggerate' just now because one change has been not dramatic but gradual: the putting of death into retirement, in every sense of the word. If you looked at the presentation of 'Dombey and Son' on television's *Children's Hour* programme you saw a world where child death was a necessary part of experience even for the most privileged groups in the world's most industrialized country. Each generation has seen a lessening of its incidence, until now the least privileged group in 1970 knows less of the necessity of child death than did the most privileged group in 1870. Now you can arrive at the age of 40 without ever having seen death.

Another change *has* been dramatic and sudden: the present generation in Britain is not exposed to the necessity of death by war. For two years no British soldier has been killed in action in any part of the world.[1] Compare this with the experience of those born between 1890 and 1900: almost a million men of that generation were killed in World War I, and vast numbers died in the epidemics which followed it. Again, consider the experience of the generation born in this century before 1925: a whole nation was mobilized for World War II, which indeed brought fewer casualties than did its predecessor but which was even more broadly involving – it exposed the entire civilian population to the possibility of death.

[1] This was true prior to the troubles in Northern Ireland. It is still true that middle class adolescents lack any such experience: those who are killed in Northern Ireland are working class volunteers.

Today, with the ending of national service, members of the present generation need know nothing of war, and – what is more important – they need know nothing of the disciplines of war. They do not learn war any more. The notion of the need for intense discipline in order to survive is quite alien to them, whereas the previous generation knew discipline and the struggle to survive as intimate personal experiences.

Yet there remains one sense in which the present generation does know more about war than any generation before it: it has access to television. We live in peace, but we are surrounded by war. We have war as an accompaniment to clearing away the tea things. No wonder some young people are appalled by the contrast!

I cite another statistic about the necessity of death: nobody has been hanged for murder in Britain in the past eight years. A small point, you may say, but it is a big indicator about how we in modern society are beginning to *feel* about the treatment and the understanding of criminality. The disciplines of society's judgment on the criminal are altering. I signed petitions for abolition of the death penalty and for alteration of the law against homosexuality. But what I signed for, my students take for granted.

Work: Privilege or Burden?

So much for the end of the necessity of death: early death, death in war, death by hanging. What about the necessity of work? It would be a gross exaggeration to say that 35 years ago people wanted work and couldn't have it, whereas now it is offered to them and they don't want it. Nevertheless, for most of the years lived by Britain's 21-year-olds today unemployment has been only between 1 and 2 per cent. Young people are keen on slogans, but 'the right to work' isn't one of them. The over-35s, and even more so the over-50s, worked to survive, whereas nowadays if you are among the young you are not satisfied unless the work you do allows for expression of your personality. One generation asked for a slot to get into, the next generation is asking to get out of a slot. The disciplines of survival have grown weaker on the industrial front; just as they have on the war front.

I don't lament any of this, but I do notice its consequences. First, because young people know little of the disciplines of survival (apart, that is, from the minor disciplines of school examinations) they do not know much about *cost*. They assume as a matter of course what older people had to pay for; they assume that you can have cakes and eat them too. And the more older people remind them of cost the more they don't want to know about it. That applies to the last war, as to everything else ('I don't *want* to know what you did in the war, Daddy'). No doubt this attitude is much better than that created by living off a diet of films about the war, but it just so happens that the older generation paid a lot for what the 21-year-old sometimes takes for granted.

In a much less dramatic way the previous generation conceived of higher education as a privilege to be bought at a *cost*; the present one conceives of it as an automatic right: 'Jude the Obscure' has gone into total obscurity. And whereas an examination used to be seen as a discipline leading to public recognition of excellence, it is seen today as a somewhat untrustworthy imposition designed to put one into yet another slot.

Revolution – and the Aftermath

So far I have said nothing about politics. I hope nobody supposes that the present generation consists largely of young political extremists; in fact, the real radical generation was the one which voted in the government of 1945, and they are now in their 40s. All our evidence shows that in most matters the younger generation is not wildly unconventional. There remains, however, a significant minority, and that minority is at its strongest in the British universities.

The Labour government of 1945 was the one which began to disband the British Empire, which established the welfare state, which nationalized a considerable segment of British industry. That welfare state required a vast bureaucracy: social justice had to be *administered*, and it needed careful planning. Yet bureaucracy, administrative efficiency and planning are just what many young people fear. They want something more personal, more creative, more immediate. The welfare state and its benefits are something they largely take for granted; running it can be left to dull, unimaginative bureaucrats. *Their* souls are too precious for that kind of thing; if they want to abuse somebody they call him a bureaucrat. They have about as much time for the administrative details of socialism as an Old Testament prophet would have for the administrative details of municipal balance sheets. 'The letter killeth and the spirit giveth life.' They do not learn war any more; the spirit giveth life.

There is another difference between the old radicals and the new: the really extreme socialists of 30 years ago admired the Soviet Union. They knew of a Beulah Land – 'a happy land, far away'. When Russia ceased to be our ally many of those people still held that *the* revolution had been successful in Russia. They could still talk about 'Soviet Russia: a New Civilization'. Any evidence to the contrary was the invention of the wicked capitalist press. Khrushchev's revelations and Hungary – let alone Czechoslovakia – ended all that; it was as if the pope had denied he was a Roman Catholic. The old communists became like orphans without a father figure. In addition, they were stigmatized as people who had defended what turned out to be an appalling tyranny. The collapse of the communist utopia in Russia left the radicals nowhere to go, or forced them to seek new models in Cuba and China.

In any case, outside the Soviet Union Marxism itself began to drop its claims that one day the working classes in the West would rise against exploitation, or that the West would stagger from crisis to crisis, with the working class growing steadily poorer. It even began to drop the more dogmatic elements in the materialist interpretation of history; consider this quotation from the Austrian communist Ernst Fischer: 'It is now the *spiritual and intellectual* agencies which are becoming of prime importance in the processes of change.' Radical thought began to turn to the *spiritual* deprivation it believed was due to capitalist society and to what it held to be the exploitation of the Third World, of the underdeveloped countries. It turned to the poor in spirit here and to those who were simply poor elsewhere. Vietnam became the symbol of that spiritual blindness and of that exploitation. And when a British Labour government showed every evidence of acquiescing in Vietnam, of being as bureaucratically minded as ever and of having forgotten all about the revolution – that proved the end.

When the Cost Is Forgotten

So it was that the radicals of the Sheltered Generation found themselves all dressed up for the revolution and almost nowhere to go. For the older generation it was a triumph to have achieved peace and affluence, but for the younger generation the so-called peace was only a supine tolerance of evil – crying peace when there was no peace – and the affluence a gross materialism which stifled the spiritual and creative potential of man. The miracles achieved by the older generation, even the scientific miracle of going to the moon, became stale commonplaces for its children. Indeed, even the preoccupation with science could be seen as a wrongheaded concern with the material, a perverse worship of 'things'. So it was that the radicals at Essex University publicly burned a motor car as a symbol both of affluence and of technocracy. In other words, the fathers had created the fortunes which enabled the sons to go and play at being St. Francis. And one must admit that for most of them 'play' is the apt term: few have much intention of actually embracing holy poverty. They will stand up for the poor of the world and at the same time demand that their grants be increased. They will condemn the capitalist system and be annoyed if they are not offered £2,000 a year on graduation.

Those who have no notion of 'the cost' do not expect even the revolution to involve much by way of discomfort. Those who cannot really envisage what discipline is can hardly realize that revolution requires planning and control. Our present radicals are ready for words, symbols, big spiritual exhibitions (especially those which get broadcast on the media), but not for the hard grind required to achieve genuine social change. It is easier to drop out with a gesture of hostile inadequacy and blame 'the system' for your own shortcomings.

All this makes the situation in the universities especially difficult. For universities involve intense intellectual discipline, and they have a tradition of subjecting the sayings of the prophets – even student prophets who look as if they have spent too long in the wilderness – to the light of reason. Thus, not only do you have revolutionaries who have been too sheltered to achieve anything concrete by way of revolution, but university students who prefer self-expression and prophecy to the disciplines of reason. In other words, you have student revolutionaries who can do little else in real terms except revolt against study. They would like to turn the world upside down but can succeed only in turning the university upside down. It seems that if we don't have revolution in the state and can't find religion in the churches we have to have revolution and religion in the university. A university teacher is now busy with revolution and religion as *well* as with science and arts; it's a full-time job.

'Doing Your Own Thing'

I want to conclude by saying something more about the religious aspects of contemporary dissatisfaction, but I am going to follow the example of the Sunday newspapers and touch on sex before I turn to religion. Let me remind you of what I said earlier about how some of the younger generation object to being put into slots and arranged in categories. That means they don't want to feel and act in a certain way just because they are biologically labelled male and female, because society says that males are chivalrous, realistic, philistine and decisive while females are emotional, dependent, artistic and domestic. The older type of woman radical tried to eliminate these differences by looking like and acting like a male; perhaps she wore mannish clothes and cut her hair short. Now members of both sexes wear what they like and let their hair grow in whatever profusion nature dictates. It's part of being natural, of being *yourself* whatever your official sex.

This doesn't mean – so far as one knows – that today's young have been desexed. They are still male and female, and their clothes don't let you forget it. The point is that though they are really male and female they don't conform to any stereotype or any conventional idea of what is *really* masculine and what is *really* feminine behaviour. They don't accept any conventional notion of what a man ought to be and what a woman ought to be.

Notice another difference between the old and the new radicals: the older radical was inclined to believe in birth *control*. But control is connected with discipline, with allowing the newly emancipated woman a chance to go out to work, to take up a profession. Now, however, you must 'do your own thing', and if that means getting pregnant then you just get pregnant. One mother in north London put it this way: 'My daughter says all the girls in her form *want* to get pregnant and I tell her to get her A levels first; time to be pregnant when you've got your A levels.'

If this situation arises with regard to new life, it also arises with regard to death. All through history we have lived *under the necessity of birth and the necessity of death.* Another north London mother said: 'I've told Simon precisely what the effects of drugs are. I told him which were ultimately lethal and suggested he warn his classmates. He told me they knew the drugs were lethal – that's why they did it.' In other words, they *choose* life and they *choose* death. That's the most drastic way of doing your own thing there is!

The Kingdom of Heaven: A Costly Vision

Here is where religion comes in, as it always does when you speak of birth, death, necessity and choice. For underlying all the current ferment is the feeling that life is too planned, too impersonal, too unchosen, too unlived, as well as materialistic. Some of today's youth don't want a planned career; they seek rather 'richness of experience'. (Sometimes, of course, this hides the fact that what is really wanted is a career handed one on a plate without working for it. Sometimes, too, the richness of experience is sought at other people's expense). The search for experience includes a search for religious experience, but generally not at the expense of working at that experience or accepting the cramps, the disciplines, the sheer necessary everydayishness of religious institutions. Young men see visions, but they are 'switched on', 'turned on' visions. Drugs provide instant vision; the result is, as one addict put it, 'Man, when you're on that stuff you don't *do* nothing'.

For all expressions of the spirit of the times Christianity retains a necessary ambivalence. It is therefore both for and against the student movement in a way that cannot please those who see in it a new revelation. Young men see visions; they believe the letter kills; they don't learn war any more. But a spoiled and petulant fractiousness is not the same thing as that condition of childlike simplicity required to enter the Kingdom of Heaven. It is not enough to trail well advertised clouds of glory if you can't face the light of common day.

Above all, the Kingdom of God is not only instantaneous but is also achieved at staggering cost. The New Testament is built around the paradox of a completely free gift bought at an appalling price. The student movement may have (to quote one of its documents) 'stormed the Kingdom of Heaven', but the capture remains illusory so long as there is no sense of the hidden cost, of the price to be paid.

7.   R. D. Laing: Psychiatry and Apocalypse

Religious movements produce prophets and vice versa. Ronald Laing is one of the major prophets of 'The New Left' and this essay tries to expound and criticize his message. One of Dr. Laing's main achievements has been to establish the fashion for regarding the 'mad' as obscurely prophetic figures vicariously crucified for the sins of the merely 'normal'. He identified his fellow doctors as the pharisaic agents of 'the system'. At the same time he celebrated ecstasy and was very much a force in the contemporary movement against the kind of complex assessment of different shades of grey involved in all political activity. A few dramatic episodes provided him with a political rhetoric and a few hints about the psychic erosion of middle range institutions (like the school) did service for a political technique. This essay is essentially a defence of politics and of the role of politician against the naivité of charismatic intellectuals. Dr. Laing has since tempered his message considerably, somewhat to the disappointment of his followers. Unfortunately it seems that his new message is not a discovery of rationality or of the nature of political action but eastern inspired contemplation of the self.

Ronald Laing must be accounted one of the main contributors to the theoretical and rhetorical armoury of the contemporary Left. By the contemporary Left is meant that soft variant of the utopian urge which has jettisoned the Marx of *Capital* for the spiritual exploration of alienation, which acknowledges that capitalism 'delivers the goods to an ever increasing part of the population'[1] and therefore concentrates its attention on the salvation of the all-too-common man from what Marcuse calls 'one dimensionality'.

With the erosion of a proletarian communism, its confinement to institutional rigidity or its continuing commitment to Stalinoid

[1] *The Dialectics of Liberation*, ed. D. Cooper (Penguin, 1968), pp. 176 and 129.

deformations, one is left with a *salon* communism, whereby the Ortega y Gassets of the Left join forces with their conservative opposite numbers on the other side of high table in a lament for the regrettable tendencies of mass society. These are – to take an image of Laing's – the lonely 'survivors' in a neo-capitalist civilization which is condemned to swinish contentment; confined to the pleasures of consumption without appropriate refinement of palate. 'Consume more, live less' as one of the slogans has it. So pessimistic is this approach that hope is only thought possible by calling in a Third World to redress the balance of the two old ones.

This is the general and by now familiar picture presented by the 'soft Left', and it is the aim of this essay to locate the place of R. D. Laing within its broad syndrome of attitudes. Unfortunately the term 'attitudes' is only too appropriate, since we are confronted here by a psychological set that positively avoids careful analysis and treats the notion of fact as a treacherous bourgeois invention. The old Left did at least propose an analysis and practised a policy in relation to concrete politics. It is arguable that their analysis and their verbal rituals were as stiff, predictable and stereotyped as a Punch and Judy Show, but the outline was devastatingly clear, and their political responses were sometimes angled (however woodenly) to what was actually happening and even to what could actually be done at a given time. It was thus susceptible to criticism. The contemporary Left, if very much more amiable, is marked above all by its preference for spiritual exhibitionism. To utilize another phrase of Laing, it has given up the experience of politics in exchange for the 'politics of experience'.

The contrast between 'soft' and 'hard' Left needs to be related to a further contrast between the rational Left and the irrational Left before the first approximate placing of Laing on the map of Left-wing ideology is possible. In its origins the Left was both the party of humanity and the party of reason, and in Marxism its abstract rationality succeeded in locating itself within the movement of history and in what was held to be a rational understanding of that movement. Now, however, the contemporary revolutionary has largely lost confidence both in the movement of history and in the efficacy of reason. The former development is mostly gain, the latter almost entirely loss.

The contrast between the rational and the irrational Left has a long history, though the contemporary drift to irrationalism and to subjectivism is particularly strong. In the present century in Britain it is possible to trace a continuous counterpoint between rationalism and romanticism within the non-communist Left; between, that is, the argued politics and articulated policies of a Bertrand Russell and the gentle apolitical withdrawals of the *gemeinschaftlich* anarchist. What Russell proposed still retained an affinity with the attitude of the hard Left in being at least a kind of politics. However much marred by the silliness of great minds, it assessed certain kinds of situation, and proposed what looked like remedies.[2]

What the romantic anarchists proposed was an end to politics, a generalized condemnation of western industrial society which sometimes had religious or mystical overtones and betrayed more than a penchant for what lies behind the famous phrase 'Civilization: its cause and cure'. Lacking either a developed sociology or an articulated politics, these anarchists tended to concentrate on the liberation of the repressed psychology produced by civilization and its discontents, or on the achievement of that liberation through sex, art and aesthetic education. Herbert Read was one of the most attractive examples of those who lay within this band of feeling and attitude. D. H. Lawrence, the archetypal contrast of Russell, provides another exemplar. 'How beastly the bourgeois is!' But whereas in the historical dramas constructed by the hard Left the bourgeois played a definable role in the predictable mechanics of the plot, for the romantic anarchists he was simply the object of ritual cursing, an all purpose stand-in for Beelzebub.

There are, of course, innumerable varieties of romantic anarchism, and not all of it is harmless artistic alienation: irrationalism can embrace both the mystique of creation or the mystique of destruction and nihilism. It can even claim to combine both, as in the slogan 'creative vandalism'. For some people destruction must precede cleansing. There is thus a hard Left as well as a soft one among the romantic anarchists which can be traced to Bakunin, to

[2] See the analysis of the political attitudes of rationalists like Russell and Kingsley Martin to the pre-war crises in my *Pacifism* (1965).

Durutti's Barcelona and to Sorel's *Reflections on Violence*.

Another point: mystique is not far removed from mysticism. This has meant that the romantic anarchism of the Left, particularly in its soft variant, has always included an interest in those religions with a weak component of rationalism. Roman Catholicism is an allowed option, not because it is irrationalist (clearly it is not) but on account of its symbolic richness, its partial dissociation from industrial civilization and its margin of mystical experience. Thus Herbert Read once declared that in the last analysis he stood with Pascal and Simone Weil and not their opponents, and the very names cited indicate that Catholicism itself has never been quite certain about this particular margin. No doubt that fact provides an additional attraction for the temperamentally heterodox. But beyond Catholic mysticism there has been the attraction of experiential cults from Eastern religions, and of Zen, not to mention the various mind-expanding drugs which have simultaneously served to release weary souls from the chains of everyday technical rationality and from the bondage of industrial society.

At any rate, on the 'soft' side of romantic anarchism, where R. D. Laing is mainly to be located, subjectivism, personalism, mysticism and creativity are in, whereas positivism and rationalism are out. The predominant style is not 'honourable argument': instead it is gnomic, testamental and confessional. The following paragraphs from Laing are perhaps the quintessence of both style and attitude. The first begins with a quotation from Jules Henry:

> If all through school the young are provoked to question the Ten Commandments, the sanctity of revealed religion, the foundations of a patriotism, the profit motive, the two-party system, monogamy, the laws of incest, and so on . . ., there would, says Laing, be such creativity that society would not know where to turn. He goes on: Children do not give up their innate imagination, curiosity, dreaminess easily. You have to love them to get them to do that.[3] Love is

[3] Something of what Laing means by love may correspond with the situation noted by D. Cooper in *Psychiatry and Anti-Psychiatry* (1967) where a mother makes statements suggesting independence and by gestures shows that she is afraid to attempt to implement the suggestion. Love in this sense can destroy the loved one by pre-defining all alternatives as wrong in one way or another.

the path through permissiveness to discipline: and through discipline, only too often, to betrayal of self.

Here is the second quotation:

> And immediate experience of, in contrast to belief or faith in, a spiritual realm of demons, spirits, powers, Dominions, Principalities, Seraphim and Cherubim, the Light, is even more remote. As domains of experience become more alien to us, we need greater and greater open-mindedness even to conceive of their existence.[4]

This is the style and the atmosphere. It is in milieux which invoke visitation by indiscriminate ecstasy that Laing's writings have provenance, and it is in a period characterized by Aleister Crowley redivivus that they resonate.

R. D. Laing was born in 1927 in Glasgow, educated at a grammar school and at Glasgow University. The flyleaves tell us that he graduated as a doctor in 1951 and became a psychiatrist in the Army for two years. He then held various posts at Glasgow Royal Mental Hospital, at the Department of Psychological Medicine at Glasgow University and the Tavistock Clinic (1957–61). He worked for the Tavistock Institute of Human Relations and has been Director first of the Langham Clinic and then of the Kingsley Hall Clinic in London since 1962. At the Tavistock Institute he concentrated initially on research on schizophrenia and the family. From 1961 to 1963 he held a fellowship of the Foundations Fund for Research in Psychiatry. So much for mere external biography.

The main writings of Laing are *The Divided Self* (1960), *The Self and Others* (1961, revised edition 1969) and *The Politics of Experience* (1967), which consists largely of miscellaneous writings from the years 1964–7. He collaborated with his fellow psychiatrist David Cooper in *Reason and Violence* (1964) which examines Sartre's principal writings between 1950 and 1960. He also collaborated with Aaron Esterson in *Sanity, Madness and the Family*, Vol. I, *The Families of Schizophrenics* (1964) and with H. Phillipson and A. R. Lee in *Interpersonal Perception* (1966). Both Laing and

[4] *The Politics of Experience* (1967), p. 60.

David Cooper helped to organize the Congress on the Dialectics of Liberation, at the Round House, Chalk Farm, in 1967, which resulted in twenty-three gramophone records and a book of the same name edited by Cooper, Laing contributed to those records; his piece in the book entitled 'The Obvious', and Cooper's Introduction, illustrate how closely linked their thinking is.[5]

A broad although ultimately unreal distinction needs to be made between Laing's work as a psychiatrist, which seems to be best represented in *The Divided Self*, and his politics. It is not a prime concern of the present essay to evaluate his psychiatric work, except insofar as the leading ideas of the psychiatric school he represents are connected with his political attitudes and also insofar as the professional perspectives deriving from psychiatric training of whatever school often seem to lead to sociological and political naïveté. Clearly a discussion of this latter could develop into a full-scale sociological critique of psychiatric perspectives on social processes which is not appropriate here but which is clearly much required. All that can be attempted here is a brief summary of Laing's methodological prescriptions, and some indication of his major substantive ideas as a psychiatrist. That done, we may pass to an analysis of the broad syndrome of attitudes, and especially religious elements, embodied in Laing's work, notably as illustrated in *The Politics of Experience*.

The main methodological prescriptions of Laing are broadly of a kind with which the present writer is in sympathy. These are mostly and perhaps appropriately addressed to psychoanalysts rather than to social scientists, and are not so much new in psychoanalysis as inadequately disseminated among the general public interested in such issues. One thinker who illustrates these trends is Binswanger,[6] and he is only one of a number of theorists to whom Laing is indebted. By methodological prescriptions is meant not so much therapeutic techniques as the fundamental therapeutic strategy and personal stance taken up by the analyst in consequence

---

[5] cf. D. Cooper, *Psychiatry and Anti-Psychiatry* (1967).

[6] cf. D. Cargello, *From Psychoanalytic Naturalism to Phenomenological Anthropology* (Daseinsanalyse). 'From Freud to Binswanger', in *The Human Context*, Vol. 1, No. 1, August 1968.

of his basic assumptions about the nature of the human entity and about the status of the notion of 'person'. However, this will clearly have its impact on what one considers therapeutically and *ethically* appropriate techniques.

Perhaps Laing's position is best summarized in his own remark that one does not *have* schizophrenia, in the same way as one has the measles, one *is* schizophrenic. A succinct statement of his position is to be found on pp. 25–26 of the Introduction to *Reason and Violence*, in some paragraphs where he is discussing both Sartre's position and his own on the limits of psychoanalysis. Laing argues that at a certain point in the process of explanation some psychoanalysts cease to make their observations within the context of mutual exchange between persons and assume a one-sided superiority of objective external judgment towards the condition of the patient as if he were a mere biological organism. Both the personal relationship and 'the person' disappear.

There are several different points encapsulated here, and some confusion. For example, there is no necessary relation between stepping into an objective role for the purpose of 'judgment' and losing the reciprocity of a relationship. Indeed, there must be *some* assumption of superiority which the analyst will take up in his role as specialist in psychological dynamics, otherwise he is simply interacting with the other person. This need not be the almost absolute assumption characteristically made (say) by a consultant in relation to biological disease, since the patient is always himself experienced in what it is to be a human and often acquires insight comparable in kind if not usually in degree to that possessed by the analyst. The patient may even, in particular instances and in relation to particular aspects, have superior insight.

Presumably Laing is not objecting to the assumption that on the average and at the margin the psychoanalyst is more experienced and in a sense more objective than the patient, and therefore must on occasion step back for a 'review' on the basis of that experience, objectivity and detachment. Moreover, a doctor may recognize how marginal the superiority of his experience and how frail and partial his objectivity while not wanting to trumpet the fact to patients who are often specialists in using such admissions as means of avoiding whatever fragments of the truth the analyst has managed to acquire. He may also legitimately restrict the degree of reciprocity and involvement which he allows himself, since he, too, has to survive.

Yet there are real dangers here to which Laing points, though it is regrettable that some of his criticisms are not more specific. For example, the psychoanalytic profession is not only expert at the game of 'tails I win, heads you lose', not only curiously indifferent to external fact such as perfectly genuine threats and difficulties, not only often oblivious to ongoing social situations, but also protects itself far more than mere personal or professional survival requires in terms of a group of ploys designed to cover the extent of professional failure. These ploys are not anything very much to do with treating people as things or with biological reductionism or anything so grandiosely perverse, but are simply the verbal mechanisms for coping practically with patients, for the reduction of proliferating involvements and for the safeguarding of medical prestige. In a way one feels that Laing prefers to concentrate on the grandiose perversity to the neglect of these unhappy mundane truths. Perhaps the exploration of the personal and professional defects which psychoanalysts share with the rest of us has less éclat than accusing them of misconceived ontology, and of treating persons as things.

Just as there is no necessary relation between elements of objectivity assumed for purposes of review and the loss of genuine reciprocity, so there is no necessary connection between either of these things and treating persons as biological entities, although there may be a necessary connection in reverse, insofar as those with a biologically and neurologically reductionist approach must find it difficult to achieve a full recognition of the equality involved in person-to-person relationships. Insofar as psychoanalysts do take up biological reductionism, Laing is surely right in pointing out that it explains all and explains nothing:

It explains all in the sense that . . . ultimately perfected biochemical and neuro-physiological techniques, and carefully delineated instinctive units of behaviour, will account 'correlatively' for every

72

possible 'psychic drive' that can be thought up. Meanwhile the person, his purposes and choices (his 'project') have disappeared: his ongoing mental life has been explained out, stultified with 'fetishised pseudo-irreducibles'.

As Laing says, 'It is only through the discovery of a freedom, a choice of self-functioning in the face of all determinations, conditioning, fatedness, that we can attain the comprehension of a person in his full reality.'

All that is well said, though those of us who are not doctors or psychoanalysts can only wonder that those who are should discover so painfully what the rest of us are not tempted to forget: that people are, after all, people. Most human beings do not require to be reassured that a person is a person by a long détour through the more verbose, pretentious and obscure German philosophers in the existentialist and phenomenological tradition. Maybe such trials are reserved as necessities for those who specialize in the science of persons, since they, it seems, have a special facility (not to say training) in forgetting what the rest of humanity remembers without thinking about it. Yet no doubt we *do* need to think about these matters: to establish as part of a carefully articulated phenomenology and ontology the validity of personal life qua personal life, independent of our unreflective awareness of it or as imparted to us through the partly unspoken assumptions of humanist and religious traditions. A philosophical détour which articulates what one always knew is not a waste of time, and the emphasis achieved by Laing in so doing is important.

Yet it *is* an emphasis, and at times so emphatic and careless as to be absurd. Presumably what he is saying amounts to an assertion that the interpenetration of levels of analysis from physics and chemistry to existential philosophy does not destroy the independent validity of each level in its own terms or render them reducible to each other. Presumably he is also saying that reductionist assumptions lurking in the medical mind lead doctors to resort more frequently than is appropriate to drugs and to physicalist methods of dealing with particular problems, such as prefrontal surgery and electric treatment. Occasionally he bothers to state this position in a qualified and commonsense form,[7] but at other times the assault on his own profession must seem so extreme as to prevent fellow-doctors hearing what he has to say. Thus: 'Doctors in all ages have made fortunes by killing their patients by means of their cures. The difference in psychiatry is that it is the death of the soul' (*The Dialectics of Liberation*, p. 19).

Laing's second main point with respect to methodological prescription concerns the relevance of the social context in interpreting individual psychology. This leads in two different directions: one is to establish the relevance of social context in any explanatory model of behaviour and the other involves a philosophical issue insofar as the positivistic abdication from value judgments prevents one seeing how the psychoanalyst is in his whole mode of operation expressing and executing the values of society. The latter point is linked with the issue already mentioned in relation to physicalist methods: an executioner dealing with crime by the rope does not absolve himself by declaring that ethical judgments are not his business. But the analogy is very partial, and in any case methods do not need to be physicalist for the essential point to be made that the psychoanalyst may act as an agent of current values by defining madness within the terms set by his society, thus failing to observe the partial responsibility of the mechanisms and institutions approved by that society for the genesis of mental disorder, overlooking the valid protest lurking behind the supposed abnormality, and assisting the patient to acquiesce again in the mad routines of supposedly normal people. This is an important point, however much overstated.[8]

The point about the relevance of the social context is also

---

[7] *The Divided Self* (1965), pp. 22–23. 'I am not here objecting to the use of mechanical or biological analogies as such, nor indeed to the intentional act of seeing man as a complex machine or animal. My thesis is limited to the contention that the theory of man as person loses its way if it falls into an account of man as a machine or man as an organismic system of processes.'

[8] Occasionally even the overstatement is avoided, e.g. on pp. 90–91 of *The Politics of Experience* where he suggests his main purpose is to *loosen* any assumption that the psychiatrist is right and the patient wrong.

genuinely helpful, but it suffers like almost all psychiatric excursions into sociology from excessive universalism. Let us take Laing's wholly acceptable remark about men qua men ultimately being free, choosing as well as 'chosen'. He both asserts this as a universal truth about the human person as such and refers to the nature of capitalist society as being a near-universal social context in which that freedom is deformed. Unless he appeals to contemporary communist society as *not* implicated in such deformations, which seems an unlikely and certainly an unpersuasive recourse, he is saying that developed society as such is a universal context within which freedom is distorted. Indeed, where he appeals to an alternative type of society he actually looks back to periods notorious for their deformation of the possibility of freedom, actually postulating in one instance a decline over the past thousand years. Since he firmly indicates no concrete milieu where deformations do *not* occur, one suspects that his category of society is not limited at all, even when it appears to have special reference to capitalist society: it is society *tout court* in all its historical manifestations hitherto which is at fault. *Vide* Freud. Thus we have two universals, the universality of freedom and the universal repressiveness of society as such.

Now it is worth asking here whether men are more or less free according to the *variations* in their social milieu, within societies as well as between them. It has been suggested, for example, that the British working class is a less 'free' milieu than the middle class because it lacks the dramaturgical skills and appropriate 'role distance' (in Goffman's sense) to exercise its freedom. Without endorsing so gross a contrast it remains true, surely, that given milieux (within the overall repressiveness of society as conceived by Laing) do make freedom more or less accessible, so that the experience of a person in the one milieu may lead him or her to have that margin of desire to exercise freedom and therefore climb by beneficent spirals out of a psychological cul-de-sac. Conversely another person may lack just that margin and by parallel vicious spirals reach a point where he is literally without option – where he may say, quite correctly, there is no way out.

Such examples do indicate both the relevance of a milieu *much* more specific and particular than society as such (though clearly this plays its part too as an overall environment) and also the possibility of losing one's freedom, in some cases entering a vicious spiral very early in the process of life such that no human mercy or grace can save one or elicit one's free choice. Personally, I would agree with Laing that freedom is a universal option of humanity, but I would also want to know whether that affirmation, as stated by Laing, takes adequate account of the variation in its availability. At what levels of analysis is it universal, at what levels variable?

There is a subsidiary point which arises here and has some relevance to Laing's politics insofar as those people who are burdened with a metaphysic of freedom frequently ignore or despise the concrete variations in the institutionalization of liberties. Just as a psychiatrist may proceed with a crude dichotomy of the individual and society which ignores the variable intermediate institutional network from society to society, so philosophers in the pursuit of genuine individual freedom despise the variations in stabilized liberties. British society, no doubt through a concatenation of favourable circumstances, has been relatively successful in the institutionalization of liberties, yet Laing's criticisms presumably apply to it with equal vigour as to anywhere else, and, since he lives here, with added emotional violence. In short, the denunciatory style of radical psychiatrists touched by existential philosophy is likely to be indiscriminately global, whereas there are, after all, seven circles both in hell and in heaven.

The points just made have been related to the variable cultural context of personal freedom and of institutionalized liberty, but they also can relate to Laing's general attempt to bring the social context into account as contributing to explanation of psychological phenomena. Laing does, of course, speak of the socialization provided by the family, and very occasionally by the school, as agents of the general socializing process emanating from global society. But he gives almost no impression whatever of the hierarchy of status and class, the processes of aspiration, of mobility and peer-group formation, and all the vastly differentiated milieux in terms of cultural pattern from one area to another, town and country, north and south. He may describe very well a highly generalized social process such as the mechanisms of gossip and scandal by which everybody is caught up in a situation which thereby acquires its own autonomous momentum because each person is primarily concerned about what the other thinks. But while he refers to persons and to groups and to society, there is little particularized social and historical location[9] through which the universal processes have to be channelled if they are to be truly explanatory.

This is perhaps more a complaint about psychiatry as such than about Laing, but it does indicate why the jeremiads and lamentations in which he engages refer so much and so indiscriminately to 'the society', 'the family', 'the school' and so on. Since he seems not personally to have rejected the family, this suggests that some families in certain circumstances are better than others. The question is: which? By always referring to institutions in general, his work is a triumph of masterful evasion.

Moreover, the generality of his work also weakens his remarks about sociology, in that sociology simultaneously aspires to adequate generality and adequate particularization. Laing's concentration on *the* group or on *the* society leads him to draw conclusions either from reading the social psychology of groups or from very abstract considerations of *the* nature of society. His comments on sociology contain very occasional slanting references to Parsons and Durkheim, but any serious acquaintance with the vast literature on the explanation of all the varied institutional patterns of modern society, or for that matter with the equally enormous literature discussing what are among his major interests – objectivity, internal personal knowledge, etc. – seem entirely lacking. While he rightly criticizes Sartre for attacking sociology on the basis of fragments from Lewin (a social psychologist) and Kardiner (a 'cultural' psychoanalyst), Laing is engaged in precisely the same exercise himself.[10]

This is equally evident in his plea for an evaluative stance and an enveloping 'total' perspective within which social science may

[9] cf. some comments by D. Cooper in *Reason and Violence* (1964), pp. 44, *et seq.*, on 'hierarchies of mediations'.

[10] D. Cooper and R. Laing, *Reason and Violence* (1964), p. 22.

operate. Such a plea rests on an objection to positivism, the very word 'positivism' (or 'vulgar positivism') being a 'boo-word' in certain circles. The core of this objection has already been stated above insofar as it relates to the abdication of the social scientist from judgments of value and his silent implication in a supposed consensus. This is a persistent theme to which one may return later. But first let us analyse, by way of example, the statement, 'Much social science deepens the mystification. Violence cannot be seen through the sights of positivism' (*Politics of Experience*, p. 51). This issue has been discussed in a thousand academic articles, and the proportion of social scientists accepting a crude positivism is very small, whether in denying the relevance of what Polanyi calls 'personal knowledge' or in asserting an unqualified scientific objectivity, whether in dismissing value judgment as merely emotive or in refusing to acknowledge the imperatives that should operate on the scientist qua person as distinct from the special role taken up with respect to problems at a given analytic level. Sociologists are simply determined to assert that it is important at least to note the *distinction* between 'is' and 'ought'. Ethical judgments will be none the less forceful for not being confused with scientific propositions. And similarly scientific propositions will not gain by being worked up and then stuffed as a mediate element in some totalizing synthesis, even one continuously constituted and reconstituted.[11] It is one of the major achievements of social science to loose itself from the bonds of ethical judgments and global metaphysics, *not* in order to reject the importance of ethics or metaphysics but to acquire a necessary (not merely a provisional) autonomy, a fragile but genuine independence for its own particular scientific purposes.

Having discussed certain aspects of Laing's methodological prescriptions one may very briefly note what are his substantive ideas in the field of psychiatry. Indeed, since a great deal of Laing's work has been on schizophrenia, it may be worthwhile utilizing a summary indicating his approach from *The Divided Self*, pp.

[11] *Ibid.*, Part 3, Section A.

161-4. This is perhaps the place to say that his analyses of inter-personal relations, either dyadic ones such as those between husband and wife or within the overall nexus of the family,[12] strike me as rich in insight. Such skill in understanding inter-personal relations does not of course validate his contentions *vis-à-vis* the geneticist-constitutional school with respect to schizo-phrenia, except insofar as he may quite rightly insist on the pro-visional hypothetical character of their approach, nor does such skill validate the naïve set of attitudes informing his political comment.

In schizophrenia the self is 'out of the body' and both wishes and fears to be reintegrated with it. The result is a disembodied self which may be lost in fantasy or engaged in a kind of dry 'observa-tion', or else may regard itself as essentially lost or destroyed. If the self is bent on self-destruction it may do so because what has been destroyed is then eternally safe. Alternatively it may be self-destructive because it has lost any sense of the personal right to be alive, or the ability to operate with a sense of what is due to one, even (say) the right to occupy a chair. The result is an experience of 'chaotic non-entity' whereby verbal expression acquires a quite bizarre and obscure coherence and in which the obscurity is deepened further because the schizophrenic is preserving his being from intrusion. His attempt at mad privacy is an effort to tell with-out being understood, to inform and communicate without giving anything away. To meet another person and communicate with him is to acknowledge the other's free existence and thus open up the possibility of the other treating one as a mere object. One takes no risks, because one believes that advantage will always be taken, and one may avoid any contact not only by secrecy but by an over-compliance which also expresses the sense of other people's ontological weight poised threateningly against one's own insub-stantiality. Yet at the same time one's greatest desire is to be allowed to *be*, and to be understood and accepted. The schizophrenic is knocking obscurely on the walls of the sunken submarine, terrified of the dangers involved in the upward route to safety and conscious of the steady diminution of the possibility of life within.

Now in Laing's view this is a condition, or rather an experience,

[12] As in *Interpersonal Perception* (1966).

to be investigated not primarily on an individual basis but within a social context, notably the context of family dynamics, and these constitute a complete pattern of interaction, processes and structure. Sometimes his focus of understanding is the family, though at other times he seems to suggest that one may conceive of a kind of primary network of some twenty to thirty people within which schizophrenia is to be treated. Neither the family nor this group ought to be regarded as a pathological organism, since the problem must be viewed as an intelligible outcome of people's intentions and actions (praxis), however much the resultant processes acquire an autonomy of their own. The schizophrenic within the family and within the wider group exists to conduct its tensions, to take the brunt of its 'unlived living' and bear the weight of its crazy structure for the rest. Perhaps one might even say that 'one dies for the people' in that the rest achieve a kind of corrupt and desperate viability through the sufferings of the chosen one. In David Cooper's words, 'Most people who are called mad and who are socially victimized by virtue of that attribution . . . come from family situations in which there is a desperate need to find some scapegoats, someone . . . to take on the disturbance of each of the others, and in some sense, suffer for them.'

The basic unit of interaction is dyadic, 'I' and 'You', and what happens in all the possible combinations of 'persons' in the family or beyond it can be partly illustrated in the basic interaction of personal perspectives. These constitute a kind of spiral based on how 'I' look in the view of 'the other'. As Laing puts it, this takes the form of 'I like you; you like me but I do not know that you like me; however I do know that you know I like you; and I do not know that you do know that I do not know that you like me'. This does not necessarily lead to withdrawals, but it is clearly potent with 'mismatched interpretations, expectancies, attributions and counter-attributions'[13] and is particularly relevant to understanding the various circles of misunderstanding, desolation, fear and corrosion into which husband and wife relations frequently fall.[14]

[13] *Interpersonal Perception* (1966), pp. 21 and 38.
[14] Cf. R. D. Laing, H. Phillipson and A. R. Lee, 'The Spiral of Perspectives', *New Society*; November 10, 1966.

These are, if you like, the basic notions: schizophrenia as a problem of personal ontology and threats to the affirmation of personal being; the 'mad' person as essentially 'bearing' the condition of the group; and the 'spiral' of potential misunderstanding informing all interlocking personal relations, but most dramatically of all perhaps, the dyad of husband and wife.

Such a brief account, however inadequate, does allow us to move on to an analysis of the underlying personal attitudes of Laing, since the fact that he sets a particular type of 'abnormal' experience within a social context, coupled with a suspicion of the psychiatrist as representing an undesirable society, allows him to question both the abnormality of the supposedly mentally ill and the normality of the society which is the context of the illness. Indeed it is perhaps central to Laing's position that modern society attempts to turn every child into a conformist and in so doing deprives the child of its potentialities and creativity, devastating its being with the chains we choose to call love. The child has gradually to be converted to a treason against itself by making a pact with the madness of society. And in this process the schizophrenic may be the one who cannot suppress his instincts enough to perform the much-solicited treason. The psychiatrist is not so much the objective representative of health as the corrupt solicitor, the secret agent of society whose *modus operandi* is tainted by precisely the ills he attempts to heal. (Those who do not view patients as persons depersonalize themselves.)

Here one must turn to a group of ideas and attitudes which provide a bridge passage between his psychiatric stance and his politics: they are contained in the notion of the 'mystification of violence'. For Laing, a central element in the broader task of 'demystification' is an attempt to 'demystify' violence, and the essence of this task is to recover access to that direct experience which socialization so successfully violates and destroys. Socialization, for him, is the local agent of that canalized institutional violence which is located in central government and which stalks ociety cloaked in the language and unspoken assumptions of the mass media. Socialization is the first and primal violence against the person which can only be met by projecting violence on to others, acting violently towards them and justifying oneself by attributing violence to them. *It is this view of socialization which links the experience of the family to politics, psychiatry to global issues, approaches to upbringing and pedagogical method to Vietnam.*

For people of this mind, all delimitation of issues, all academic division of scholarly labour, and all attempts to view phenomena objectively from a variety of specialized perspectives at different analytic levels, are part of a policy of divide in order to rule. There can be no taking apart of Humpty-Dumpty even in order to put him together again: the question is, as Humpty-Dumpty himself said, 'Who is master?' The appeal of this to the kind of young person looking for quick global answers, impatient with the requirements of careful study, and armed with a drifting paranoid suspicion of all authority, is obvious. The psychology of identifying a malevolent 'Them', which he describes, is unusually well developed in his followers.

Global accusation, like libel and rumour, is easy: refutation, like art, is long and difficult. There is no answer to a grain of truth eked out by indiscriminate misrepresentation except a disciplined understanding. It would take too long; but one can at least begin by pointing to the central assumption, derived from Rousseau, that man as man is originally innocent, and civilization, especially modern civilization, the focus of original sin. Incidentally, it is interesting that this assumption links Laing with another large success in the field of commercial publishing: the type of egregious ethological speculation represented by *The Human Zoo* and *The Naked Ape*. In short there are those who see human institutions as dykes canalizing a raw, variable, morally ambiguous human potential into the fructifying ways of civilization, and those who see those institutions as barriers to a flood of inherent generosity, innate humanity and abounding creativity. Laing is of the latter.

That said, it is instructive to look more closely at what appears to be a very confused discussion (pp. 50–53 of *The Politics of*

Experience) which Laing conducts concerning socialization, violence and value judgments. What he says is this. First, socialization, including moral and political socialization, is a violence against personal experience because it is socially derived and imposed rather than individually achieved. Now it is not clear how else moral perspectives can be derived in the first instance except from society, and it is even less clear that people do not, as they mature, partly transform what is so derived into a personal and critical perspective. Secondly, Laing argues that to regard animals and humans in a given scientific context as (e.g.) biochemical complexes is equivalent to a denial of their true nature as animals and persons; and such a context prevents those who adopt it from an ethical response when violence against men and animals is perpetrated.

Now there is a tiny grain of truth here, which is that a person specializing at a given level of scientific interest such as biochemistry may become so professionally deformed as to forget that what he studies is also a human being, may indeed refuse to acknowledge that in principle results may need to be reassimilated within a wider view which includes the specifically human. Humpty-Dumpty may lie shattered on the floor. It may even happen that such an attitude enters into a scientist's general moral perspective. But it happens to a certain degree to certain people, and the extent to which it does would require extensive documentation; unfortunately the techniques of the propagandist asserting the primacy of his 'genuine' human experience do not allow so wasteful an expenditure of intellectual energy in the cause of mere verification. It is more economical and more effective to say, 'Meanwhile Vietnam goes on.' And here one encounters a cheapness of effect which in Laing goes with this kind of intellectual economizing. The situation in Vietnam is too appalling, the issues too confused, the murderous intent on both sides too typical of war at almost all times, for it to be used as a catch-all riposte by those too lazy or too frenetic to engage in honourable argument.

In any case, a more appropriate intellectual economy might have been employed, since what is being said is even more simple than appears. Laing is claiming that his value judgments are rooted in his genuine experience as a human being, whereas those who disagree with him are the deluded facsimiles of over-successful socialization. He has not adequately considered the possibility that – to quote him from a different context – his opponents may be people like himself, dressed differently. They, too, may be human.

With world enough and time, it would be worth while indicating just how grossly Laing exaggerates the pressure of socialization on the child in the democratic West as compared with almost any other period or type of society. It is in fact so affected by a degree of indecision and by a measure of self-indulgent irresponsibility (backed by fashionable psychologies) about its right to socialize, that it often neglects to give those firm, compassionate guidelines within the family and the school without which the child is a flailing ego. Many children rightly suspect that absence of discipline is absence of love. Our school systems are attempting to achieve a balance between required structures and individuality: if they err it is sometimes in taking the sentimentalities deriving from Rousseau too seriously, in acceding too easily to callow cults of spontaneity. On the contrary, it is the duty of a home or school proudly and exultantly to induct a child into that incredibly rich human achievement called civilization, and into those social, spiritual and intellectual disciplines on which it is built.

It would also be worth showing that some element of mystification is inherent in every civilized social achievement, including the violence socialized, rationalized and sometimes civilized, in the state. Masked (or 'mystified') violence is often a step forward in a peaceable direction; in certain circumstances men gradually conform to their own peaceful self-portraits and are pressed by opinion to implement their misleading idealizations. Men always partially misrepresent their actions: legitimate and minimum authority can be labelled repressive violence; repression can be labelled the maintenance of civilized order. That is not surprising. Men do attempt to delude themselves and others. There are indeed certain situations where the total truth is the grossest violence and where the question is always: what is the most responsible and compassionate proportion of truth and delusion? That is as true of politics as it is of person-to-person relations. Confronted by one's own humanity and others', there is only one possibility: a relaxed compassion towards oneself and other people.

The logic of Laing's position is ultimately violent and totalitarian in spite of (or because of) its extreme libertarian gloss. Perhaps its possibilities are best illustrated by a passage from John Gerassi in *The Dialectics of Liberation* (p. 93). Gerassi presents as an alternative to Stalinism something exemplified in Cuba, where 'one way to guarantee that their people are genuinely free is not elections, is not free press, is not all the trappings of the so-called political democracy that we have, but simply to arm their people'. In short, if democracy and a free press are less genuine than they claim, the best answer is to abolish free elections and ban open comment; and the best response to militaristic tendencies is the total militarization of everybody. It is a curious consummation to the metaphysics of freedom.

This is the framework, these the plausible half and quarter-truths which are major keys to the syndrome of attitudes found in Laing. They are allied to a stress on the need for transcendence, which is in part a range of experience akin to mystical illumination which modern society is held to inhibit and denigrate and which is also an ability to see beyond the confines of one-dimensionality to another mode of social life. Since this is important, any exposition must include some reference to the religious elements found in Laing: our alienation from ecstasy and the problem of an original sin uniquely focused in capitalist society. The best way into such an exposition is to concentrate on these attitudes as illustrated in *The Politics of Experience*, and to preface them with a brief look at Laing's contribution to *The Dialectics of Liberation* entitled, *The Obvious*. The crucial point for criticism of Laing is the contrast between his politics of experience and the experience of politics.

It is 'obvious' to Laing that what is 'irrational' in the individual can be understood in the context of the family, and that the irrationality of the family is intelligible within its 'encompassing networks', and so on up to the society itself and the total social world system. Each of the wider systems pervades the smaller subsystems. There is nothing within which the irrationality of the world may be made intelligible, unless it be God, and perhaps he is mad too. Social salvation is not possible by individual conversion nor by seizing the state apparatus but by working outwards from the middle range of institutions, e.g. factories and schools. Psychiatry is the unwitting agent of a political operation against the individual, and the patients are thrown up and selected by a system of which psychiatrists are the malign solicitors. This violence against the individual is paralleled by violence on the societal scale: while the micro-system selects an individual, the macro-system selects 'them'. 'Them' currently comprise the Third World, the have-nots, the exploited. We are enabled to see the Third World as 'them' by our own misconception of what we wrongly believe to be the western desire for peace and by our faith in its vaunted democracy. We project our own unjust violence on to them, are surprised at their just violence against us, and so feel justified in destroying Vietnam.

So universal is our ignorance of and obedience to this system that the number of those surviving as human beings is minute. Socialization makes us into unwitting subjects of the system just as psychiatrists are made into its unwitting agents. The normal mode of socialization, terrorization into submission by love, repeats an endless spiral back through countless generations to the beginning. This spiral backwards is the precondition of our projecting a world composed of 'us' and 'them' in which the hatefulness of 'them' is ourselves seen in the mirror. The crux of the system is obedience resting on the generation of guilt and on the reflex of believing in the authorities. The state, the Church, the government, scholarship and science – authority and authorities – all are partners in such a morass of delusion that almost nothing can be truly known: we can only trust something deeper than ourselves, and it is most obvious that *this* is most hidden.

These basic themes are simply found on a larger scale in *The*

Politics of Experience: white western society, its governmental system, its methods of upbringing, its science and its scholarship are part of a tissue of delusion which is responsible for stereotyped divisions into 'us' and 'them', and is to blame for violence and counterviolence. We think 'they' are to blame; not at all, it is we who are to blame in the world. This is a simple diagnosis, easily achieved by standing an equally simple diagnosis on its head. The basic stratagem of this style of thinking is: if you want to know what to believe, find out what is the current consensus and turn it upside down; that way you won't necessarily be right but at least you won't inevitably be wrong. If, in addition, you hope for a hint as to what is right, listen to those whom society stigmatizes as abnormal. They've got something.

As one proceeds to document the Laingian position one can hardly help noticing two characteristics in his own work which illustrate his own analysis of what constitutes a fundamentally irrational view of the world. One is the simple stereotyping of 'us' and 'them', encapsulated in vast assertions about what people in western societies think: a grandiose simplification of all issues achieved by stigmatizing whole societies as solidary elements in 'the Enemy'. No evidence is cited, just projections about what people in the disapproved societies are projecting about 'them'. This looks like an unfortunate example of the spiral perspectives in which Laing is himself a specialist. The other characteristic is the repetition on the macro-scale of what he describes as inherent in the experience of schizophrenia on the microscale. All other types of society *except* his own have some kind of ontological root, something which may be admired, some kind of right to exist. Only that which is his own constitutes a kind of delusion, a mass of subhumanity, suffering from ontological weightlessness. There is in Laing's writing not a single word suggesting that any virtue inheres in what is his own inheritance. So total a rejection, so wholehearted a separating out of the self from the body of society, so extraordinary a fear of becoming re-attached to it by fiendish subtleties, looks like a curious analogue of the self hating what is most truly its own.[15] Perhaps the condition could be called macro-schizophrenia.

In *The Politics of Experience* the viewpoint expressed is religious not only in the chapter concerned with 'transcendental experience' but throughout. The word religious is not used figuratively: it happens to be accurate. The more extreme forms of a religious rejection of the world often result in two apparently contradictory responses both illustrated in Laing: the first is a flailing violence towards all mundane structures, all those things which for others may mediate elements of truth and personal being. Roles, institutions and everyday experience are rejected because what they mediate is not *the* Truth, because they partly mask what they partly reveal. This obsessive pilgrimage towards the Absolute may result in a total rejection of all the way-stations where other people have rested on their journey, and in an excoriating contempt for their blindness. They are the blind led by the blind. They 'scurry into roles, statuses, identities, inter-personal relations'. In other words they escape into the bolt-holes of partial sanity because they cannot bear too much sanity, just as others escape into partial madness because they have an inkling how partial the sanity found in those bolt-holes really is. Laing's choice of visionary viewpoint is allied to Eliot's 'Mankind cannot bear very much reality', but without his compassion.

The second form taken by this religious rejection of the world is silence, because the search for the Absolute has been attempted

[15] David Holbrook's criticism of Laing – 'Madness to Blame Society' (*Twentieth Century*, 2, 1969) – points to the seductive charm of blaming 'society' for everything. He also suggests that in treating schizophrenia the analyst can come to play out for himself the meanings he desperately attributes to the patient. A histrionic manner is acquired which the analyst finds increasingly real to him until he feels lost outside schizophrenic company. To get through to the patient he adopts an exaggerated pose as a fellow-sufferer which requires him to blow up the oppressiveness of social situations and act contemptuously to ordinary common life and the normal sources of identity. Having originally seen the patient as an oracle, the analyst becomes oracular. Holbrook himself describes this as an essential self-indulgence according well with the attitude 'I'm this way because society . . ., etc., etc.' Naturally this attitude is in some tension with assertions of existential freedom. cf. also P. Sedgwick 'Laing's clangs' (*New Society*, January 14, 1970).

and failed. The Truth itself was not available (or only intermit-tently) and, since all the mediate intervening half-truths have been rejected, nothing can be said. Speech is an impropriety and the structured or prepared speech is a blasphemous attempt at order when no order is possible. This is close to the Quaker experience. One must be silent concerning that which cannot be spoken. As Laing puts it, 'Black on the canvas, silence on the screen, an empty white sheet of paper, are perhaps feasible. There is little conjunc-tion of truth and social "reality".' Stylistically the only mode of expression is unprepared, unstructured, gnomic, enigmatic. There is no truth in mere knowledge, no truth in social forms, no truth in ourselves. 'We are all murderers and prostitutes . . .' Here the Quaker experience mutates back to the characteristic Calvinist experience: the total reprobation in which man as man is univer-sally implicated. Indeed, in Laing we have constant shifts between four main modes of the religious consciousness: mystical ex-perience of the *co-incidentia oppositorum*, intense prophetic violence, withdrawal into silence, into institutional and intellectual dis-solution, and total reprobation. And Laing himself, through a residual Presbyterianism, is unwilling to assert that he is one of the Elect – 'the survivors'. As he puts it: 'We who are half alive, living in the often fibrillating heartland of a senescent capitalism . . . Can we do more than sing our sad and bitter songs of disillusion and defeat?' *Super flumina Babylonis* . . . the reference appears to be to capitalism *or* to Babylon: universalized it is the essence of the religious awareness that 'here we have no abiding city'. Whether our civilization is so hostile to this awareness as he maintains, so relentlessly secular, as compared with others, is open to doubt. The nature of the dissent it is capable of producing may be taken both as its condemnation and its salvation. Laing himself con-tradicts his own thesis. It is a kind of compliment.

Although religious experience can achieve a general prophetic denunciation of a given social condition it is a poor guide to day-to-day politics. These are inevitably, and *quite properly*, conducted in a dubious half-light of more or less unhappy compromises, and to the extent that they are invaded by religion then either each shifty pragmatic compromise is papered over by religious legitimation or intimations of the New Jerusalem drive *l'homme moyen sensual* relentlessly and intolerantly towards a predestined goal. Essentially the politics of experience are no adequate guide to the experience of politics; a denunciation is not a viable policy. It is this fact that should be the basis of any critical appraisal of the type of politico-religious awareness found in Laing.

When earlier in this essay I located Ronald Laing on the fringes of the irrationalist Left there was one sense perhaps in which it was untrue. He does not explicitly embrace irrationalism, and indeed he uses the word 'irrational' to stigmatize institutions and activities of which he disapproves. However, in such instances he rarely tells us what he means by 'irrational' and one can only assume he uses the word simply as a stand-in for emotional disapproval. He can certainly be considered an irrationalist in that he finds rational and argued discussion of religious questions uncongenial, and insists that the essence of religion is ecstasy. And while it would be better to regard ecstasy as supra-rational rather than irrational, there is in Laing's whole style a *substitution* of ecstasy for argument and a disinclination to build up a sequence of ordered points, supported by carefully collected evidence, qualified in respect of this issue or that.

His method consists in random accusations and sloganized virulence, which destroys the possibility of genuine discussion. Patient refutation has to build up on a basis of carefully verified evidence, has to define its terms (whereas Laing simply prefers to use them) and eventually to build up a cumulative impression, usually in terms of more or less, of marginally this rather than that. Such a method cannot compete with a rhetorical either/or, with grossly simplified alternatives, with slogans used as an excuse for not thinking. You cannot talk with a man who throws his sincerity at you and who persistently implies that you and every other person who disagrees with him is a racialist, an anti-semite and a crass authoritarian. It is like a discussion arranged between a Pentecostalist in the pulpit and a Unitarian in the congregation: the convention within which the exchange takes place is set by the enthusiast, not by the enquirer.

Laing will not engage in rational argumentation because that is not the way converts are made. Laing is also an irrationalist in the sense that he proposes no means to achieve his vision, apart from offering vague hints about psychic subversion in the middle-range type of institution, such as the school and the university. He proposes no policies, articulates no alternatives, raises no queries about viability, weighs no costs and advantages, assesses no immediate and remote consequences. For obvious reasons: if he did, the whole visionary edifice would collapse like the baseless fabric of a dream. The old Left at least proposed a method of bringing dreams to fruition: when that method proved a nightmare the Left was reduced to the dream again and to variants of peyote. Not indeed that mankind should or can give up its dreams, but without an articulated machinery for the dream to be brought on stage it remains generalized in proclamations, embedded in rituals and confined to what can be achieved by sympathy and goodwill: in short, it remains religious. Holy Communion – by sharing bread and wine – is a symbol and sometimes also a realization of a preliminary achievement in brotherhood and a pointer to the need for extending both its fellowship and the presence at the heart of that fellowship: but it cannot substitute for the pragmatic turmoil and administrative grind and cold calculation necessary for political action. Politics cannot simply be a gospel, or else that gospel eventually declines not only into ritual but into mere ritual.

So much contemporary protest of the kind that Laing admires seems to consist of precisely these rituals and exhibitions executed by those who have no access to the idea of cost and are therefore unwilling to pay the administrative and personal costs of their gospels. For example, Laing's collaborator David Cooper refers to the schizophrenic as the author of the 'totally gratuitous crazy act' and the once-for-all 'happening' is precisely this: a negative symbol whose only point is its negation and which explodes violently into nothingness. As Laing himself might put it: a 'happening' is the negation of the negation. On the continuum running from pragmatic articulated politics to the gratuitous crazy act Laing and Cooper stand about midway, but their sympathies clearly turn towards the latter end of that continuum. They find it easy to indulge in generalized abuse of politicians, easy to sympathize with the psychotic and to regard him as less 'estranged from reality' than the politician. Yet sympathy for psychotics need not be linked to a modish contempt for politicians.

There is no more important task in defending the disciplines of civilization against writers such as Laing than the rehabilitation of the political vocation. The abuse of politicians is one of the major forms of contemporary self-indulgence. In the demonology of those who aspire to be *real human beings* (and who so often inflict their humanity indiscriminately on others) politicians are the archetypes of the straw man, drained of all ontological root. They are regarded as the prisoners of themselves and the gaolers of the rest of us. Yet in this competition for ontological supremacy perhaps even the politicians and the bureaucrats have a chance. When one considers the nature and constraints of politics there is perhaps in politicians a kind of heroism. Let us at least nominate them as competitors in the ontological stakes, alongside those traditionally easy winners, the artists and intellectuals.

The politician can be a man who wears a mask over his humanity in order the better to serve that humanity. Admittedly it is often an orthodox conventional mask: yet it could be that behind the disguise lies more humanity than in those who affect no disguises, whose appearance of open-hearted innocence depends on the proclivity for unmasking other people. In any case, many people accept the disciplines which require a mask in a certain limited area of their life, say their profession, but are able to relax into simple humanity in every other sphere of their life; others have no imperative need for masks in any area of their lives, perhaps because they have chosen just those areas of social life where the discipline of social relations can be lax and easy, where few exigencies constrict and few responsibilities congeal. The politician, however, has chosen a role where exigency and responsibility demand a mask at nearly all times.

Consider the following proposition: that the highest moral responsibility could conceivably reside in a civil servant, or a politician at the Ministry of Defence, who uses the coolest rational calculation to tread that narrow edge which is marginally closer to survival than all the alternatives. Once such a man has chosen a policy he is within certain limits committed to it, indeed knows in advance that what he has chosen may acquire a momentum which will control him. He knows it includes certain costs, may in extreme circumstances begin to include further costs which may be appalling, but which when that stage has been reached are probably (but not certainly) less appalling than the alternative costs. Perhaps such a man is a *kind* of genuine human being: willing to accept what it will be like to live with himself and with the obloquy of those not in his shoes should the worst happen.

As the consequences of his choice accumulate he becomes totally immersed in fending off the worst, and this may mean the death of his personality; nothing but a public life and an 'insane' commitment to politics. Not even the relief of an autobiographical exposition of his motives is open to him: he can only advise and act. Whatever he does now will acquire no honour in the world of those easily achieved martyrdoms undertaken in 'progressive' causes. Indeed he may have to face the obloquy of seeming to acquiesce in and abet just such a martyrdom. This kind of man accepts the need for painful struggle and refuses to inveigh easily against the structures of reality, but instead employs the highest rational cunning to play those structures as far as they can be played: this is both a creative act of his own *and* an encounter with a strange, alien, recalcitrant otherness.

His highest achievement will be a tiny victory, his normal achievement just to survive. This he will never be able openly to explain, and may have to accept the mortification of having to claim that a tiny victory was a great one. He may even acquire a reputation among the *cognoscenti* for naïve reasoning and dishonest appeals, simply because the public neither wishes to know his actual reasons nor would be willing to face the stark alternatives involved in that reasoning. It may even be that he is a man of the highest intelligence who must accept the contempt of an intelligentsia which has never tried to understand why he must appear stupid in public and appear ignorant of what he may know better than anyone. Perhaps such a man has some claim to his humanity and ours.

93

8.   Me Doctor, You Patient

The most important institutional agency of interpersonal control and social tradition is the family. Dr. Laing analyzed and attacked the constrictions of family life from the viewpoint of existential 'openness'. This part of his message very much appealed to the anomic population of semi and intermittently employed graduates and it legitimated their disorganized style of life as more authentic and genuine than that of the conventional citizenry. A horror of modern society and its complex structure of roles is very characteristic of sociology students and of people seized by the social romanticism of 'Eng. Lit.'. Hence the appeal of Dr. Laing.

This latest collection of Dr. Laing's sermons[1] will appeal to all those who follow the publications of the North London Pulpit. The rhetoric is brilliant, the expository style persuasive, the content intriguing. Unlike Dr. Cooper, his fellow preacher, Ronald Laing is not so much a prophet of the death of the family as a student of its present reality. Like the preachers of the seventeenth century he provides an analysis of the soul on its way to the Light. His text is the dominical injunction against family piety, 'Let the dead bury their dead', and his metaphors are those of awakening and rebirth.

His work is hortatory in style and content. In one sense it is – as I have written before[2] – gnomic and testamental, but in another it is most cunningly structured in the manner of the conventional sermon. For one thing it makes its impact by slight variations on

[1] R. D. Laing, *The Politics of the Family, and other Essays*, Tavistock Publications, £1·50.

[2] David Martin, 'R. D. Laing' in *The New Left*, edited by Maurice Cranston, (Bodley Head, London; The Library Press, New York).

constantly repeated themes. In the first essay one finds the following. The family consists of relations. It exists in each of its elements and nowhere else. The family is not an introjected object but an introjected set of relations. What is internalized are not objects as such but patterns of relationship by internal operations upon which a person develops an incarnate group structure. Relations are internalized and construed for significance. This family-in-common shared group presence exists in so far as each member has it inside himself. Thus in a mere II pages the basic phenomenological doctrine is hammered home: the family is not a *thing* but a more or less internalized pattern of relationships.

Similarly, the sermon technique is evident in the employment of another basic phenomenological mode: the slow preliminary exegesis of the framework of the obvious, the fundamental grammar of relationships. In the manner of Schutz he articulates the structure of the family in space and time: it is either close-knit or scattered in space, married once and now divorced in time. There is a relational grammar of we, me, you, us and them, hers, his and mine. All are members one of another as men may be members in the Party, the Nation, or the Church.

Again, sermons use analogy and word play. On page 74 Laing is discussing 'secondary transformations', that is what happens when one's inner experience has to be denied and when internal reality becomes out of phase with external definition. Wishes and memories are outlawed and excommunicated. Immediately the penal analogy takes over: the psychiatric 'mind police' are called in; they take the criminal (patient) into custody (hospitalization); he confesses by a show of insight and a therapeutic sentence is pronounced. Because his experience has been invalidated he becomes an invalid (word play almost worthy of Lancelot Andrewes or Donne).

A final characteristic of sermonizing is vagueness. One moves very slowly and deliberately at the level of personal relationships, spelling it out carefully, repeating, illustrating, and then suddenly one spirals as rapidly as a firework up to a vague outer space comprising 'the world' and 'society'. The mediating levels of all the various interstitial social spheres are traversed by the merest

TRACTS AGAINST THE TIMES

mention, and it is the total system which comes under prophetic judgment. From a discussion of familial rules which one is prevented from acknowledging (and from acknowledging, or even knowing, that one *is* so prevented) the rhetoric roars upward to the 'Western conscience' into which we are all supposed to be so tightly knit and knotted together. As he says, in a final exordium, the more we comply with the rules the more we have to break them. He completes the sermon with the proper appeal to Scripture: 'our righteousness is as filthy rags' (p. 116).

Consider for a moment another successful series of sermons: the pieces delivered by Edmund Leach under the auspices of that august presbyter, Lord Reith.[3] Certain points of comparison are worth making. Leach took as his theme the great Abelardian text '*I have said ye are gods*', and he called on us to awaken to our status as incipient godlings, masters of all we surveyed. It was yet another evangelical call to take full charge of our own destiny. Then, Leach attacked that vehicle of continuity the family, lashed out at those who obediently conformed to parental expectations, and confidently claimed that the family

> with its narrow privacy and tawdry secrets, is the source of all our discontents . . .

By this he meant the competitive pressures of status and economic emulation. He also pointed to changes in the family from an extended kinship network to a primary nucleus. Now, there is little in Laing that suggests either this important *external* history of the family or to indicate that (in another scriptural phrase) 'the love of money is the root of all evil', *Homo economicus* does not play any role on the family scene, whereas it is a fact that people *do* have jobs and that the role divisions and status tensions attendant on them *can* be crucial for the analysis of family dynamics. Perhaps Laing thinks so too but he makes almost no reference to the fact.

To be sure Leach and Laing conform to type in attacking con-

---

[3] Edmund Leach, *A Runaway World* (Reith Lectures for 1967), Oxford University Press.

formity as well as in attacking the family. This much is *de rigueur*. Laing, however, goes further. In the process of attacking conventional wisdom he succeeds in illustrating it. Not everything in Laing is conventional, and some of it is very neglected common sense – neglected at least among psychiatrists – but in certain respects (which I shall indicate below) he repeats the contemporary wisdom about being a Real Genuine, Authentic Person and about the ontological deprivation of the desiccated bureaucrats as if it were revelation. That inverts the normal practice of sermons. In conventional sermons revelation becomes platitude; in *soi-disant* unconventional sermons platitude becomes revelation.

Sermons require a congregation if not a church. The Round House at Chalk Farm (N.W.1), may be regarded as the great Tabernacle of the North London Pulpit. Hither the tribes of Judah come: the graduate proletariat, shifting from unhappy liaison to unhappy liaison, wandering from bed-sitter to bed-sitter. All the young pseudo- and sub-intelligentsia congregate on the small, windy hills of northern London, fleeing their middle-class backgrounds, affecting authentic squalor, leading the messy lives that prove their rejection of achievement and their search for *spontaneous* – and hence real – selfhood. If Laing never refers to *homo economicus* it is not surprising: a large part of his congregation is in part-time employment. This sad, voluble, resentful and intermittently employed flotsam is Dr. Laing's congregation, for whom the revelation provides a sort of validation of personal disorder by claiming it is the pre-condition of real life and creativity. The saddest thing about these people is the dreary predictability with which his disciples repeat the revelation in the name of the holy spirit of spontaneity. Dr. Laing has many creative and interesting things to say: the *epigoni* are repetitive bores.

I said above that in a special restricted sense Dr. Laing purveys conventional wisdom. The conventional wisdom is the prejudice against rules, roles and relations on the ground that they stultify the expression and achievement of the Real Self. To study the tragedies consequent on rules is not to invalidate the need for rules or the fact that equal and infinitely more numerous tragedies would arise if rules were absent. Dr. Laing somehow sets rules against authenticity, personal experience against external rite, people against a structure of relations – when, in fact, rules and roles and relations are the necessary though not the sufficient condition of any kind of authentic person.

People thrown on the random resources of the unhedged psyche are set on a path where the achievement of authenticity becomes a passion which consumes its capacity to gain its own object – or rather its own subject. Furthermore, one person's pursuit of authenticity is another person's blasted possibility. It only needs one such liberated spirit to leave a trail of other people's broken potentialities behind him.

Over-development of the aspiration towards 'the real' devalues the common, repeated, everyday in which the profoundest satisfactions can lie. Thus family life both breeds a sense of quiet desperation and suffocation *and* a common life of steady ritual, renewed confidences, demarcated privacies and deep familiarities without which people are lost souls. The familial is the familiar: that which defines, orders, and maintains the personal world. People can die within that order; they can barely live without it or without some substitute which is usually more, not less, restrictive. Moreover, many of the processes he describes are general phenomena of life operating as the necessary ground of social existence: for example partial reciprocity, focussed and restricted identifications, unacknowledged systems of rules, proffered ranges of distinctions, definitions and options, processes of prescribing not by directions but by attributions and labels. These processes have their costs, which are sometimes heavy and repressive, but they admit an amelioration in the way they operate, and *total* reciprocity, *absolute* openness and lack of demarcation are neither possible nor desirable. All viable culture is a restriction on 'world-openness', and that restriction in turn makes possible (though not inevitable) the recovery of some openness to the world. To push for *total* openness is to fall over into an inherent contradiction. Kibbutzim replace the family only by being *more* restrictive; universal communities of love rigorously exclude the outside world; rejection of any Them which is Other ends up by identifying as a sub-human Them all who do not reject that division in the way you do. I'm not sure that Laing himself does not acknowledge as much.

I have previously characterized Dr. Laing's condemnation of his own profession as exaggerated to the point where he destroys the likelihood of a favourable reception. Nevertheless, he is quite right about the deficiencies of a great deal of psychiatric practice, particularly the kind of individual therapy which inhibits wider explorations.

Thomas Hardy has a haunting poem where he describes the constant reduplication of 'the family face'. Laing documents the way in which generation after generation the fallen face of a family is projected down a hall of mirrors. He rightly draws on common observation of the way people recognize this partial re-duplication generation after generation and points out that the way this operates in any given family is often least understood by the participants. People *note* the fact of reduplication without *understanding* the process; and that process is such that it interdicts any recognition of itself. The process is only weakened by slow dilutions and the criss-crossing of one type of process by another, some of these processes being more benevolent than others. Laing does not tell us anything about *benevolent* family systems. For him particular pathology is the key to universal pathology. There is no variable incidence in the structural location of sin, unless maybe in the institutions of non-Western cultures. (When he is not condemning Society as such, the West does tend to be his particular malevolent Other.)

Laing is a *social* psychiatrist in that he does understand the structural location of illness in the family and in wider networks. This, again, is a commonsense position which the practice of too many psychiatrists denies. The extraordinary resistance of the psychiatric profession to investigating the whole familial context is remarkable even in institutions dedicated to communal therapy.

TRACTS AGAINST THE TIMES

Thus, psychiatrists may rely entirely on treatment of the individual in that they make no provision for altering the context to which the 'patient' returns, acknowledge no impact deriving from the real exigencies of social living at the time, and *avoid* alternative sources of evidence from other members of the system in which the patient is implicated. It is not merely, of course, that a parent may need treatment as much as a child but that there is a structure of relationships about which all the relevant perspectives need to be understood. To see the patient as a hall of mirrors apart from current constricting exigencies and without assessing the total distribution of psychic weights in the crazy structures in which he is implicated is, to put it correctly, a form of madness to which only a carefully trained doctor could aspire. Only the 'Me Doctor, You Patient' syndrome (to quote Eric Idle) could lead to such monstrous professional deformation. When Laing says that psychiatrists often do little more than operate a few standard myths he tells no more than the truth. No wonder that the prestige of psycho-analytical procedures exists most strongly in the social work field where it acts as a myth of professional legitimation and is uniquely low in the academic world of the social sciences.

Yet Laing does not carry his analyses far enough. The additional standard myth which he is proposing cuts off large segments of familial reality. For example, one of his primary modes of analysis is in terms of tragic drama – a Greek tragedy repeated with variations over generations in which the basic meaning is often hidden from the participants. He employs a dramatic image and aspires to study the 'scene' as it unfolds in terms of multiple refracting perspectives and the reciprocal mutations of the story proposed by the participants. But even within this dramatic mode a crucial element is lacking: comedy. If one looks at his index there is no entry under 'joke'; yet what the anthropologists call 'joking relationships' are a very important key to the 'politics of the family'.

Partly this is because what is joked about is often no laughing matter. People can convey their meaning and their understanding of the situation through the joke when no other means are open. Yet it is also because jokes are based on a sense of incongruity, and it is the disjunction between experience as felt and as defined which is Laing's primary interest. His whole analysis turns on the dire consequences of the Inner not matching the Outer, and a primary mechanism of expressing this lack of fit is the joking relationship. Indeed jokes derive from the Inner not meeting the Outer and are actually part of the richness which can result from that disjunction. One suspects that the crusade against lack of fit is a crusade against comedy. Laing's analyses describe no comedy and contain none. The family is not only a tragedy but also a comedy, and anyone sitting down with a book called *The Politics of the Family* should be anticipating something pretty ludicrous.

The approach based on the unfolding scene parallels approaches in sociology (*e.g.*, Dalziell Duncan, or ethno-methodology); and like them, it neglects segments of the external. For example, the specific semi-discrete networks of work and status and their semi-autonomous processes are largely absent from Laing's analysis. These impinge on the family, often in quite a crucial manner. I suggested above that Laing's congregation is in part-time employment, which is why his internal mode of analysis appeals to them. But many of them also know themselves to be the consequences of 'objective' external processes in the social system: their joblessness related to the over-production of graduates, their emotional difficulties related to patterns of educational striving operative in their homes, or to the status tensions reflected in their families. Thus one knows of psychiatrists who on principle avoid not only knowledge of wider networks but any sensitivity to their *specific* sociological character.

Imagine, for example, a working-class family in which the mother retains middle-class connections and therefore practices certain varieties of social withdrawal from neighbourhood ties. Imagine, also, a father deep in work and trade union activities and, to that extent, partly withdrawn from the family. Impose on these a pattern of educational striving and a particular division of roles between son and daughter whereby the son is offered partial autonomy at the price of relative insensitivity.

Thus the psychic burden of family sensitivity falls on a daughter for whom the father does not provide the necessary degree of support and contact. The daughter receives the same cues demanding educational success as the boy, but in an emotionally charged situation which cripples her so that she feels unable to meet the call to daughterly and intellectual perfection. She feels incapable of feeling and becomes immobilized. Now, at this point the 'double binds' so brilliantly described by Laing – the rules contradicted by other rules, the rules whose existence is denied, and whose denial is denied – begin to operate so that their incidence falls more on the daughter than the son.

Imagine, in addition, a psychiatrist who treats this all in terms of the father- or mother-aspect of the patient and who insists as a methodological *principle* on not knowing about, let alone understanding, the wider context of class, status, and educational striving. Consider what it must imply for a psychiatrist *not* to understand the role of educational striving in particular groups – and, in addition, to see all relationships in the wider network outside the family as pure extensions of the family images and, therefore, denuded of inherent relevance. Consider what it means if therapy is purely concerned with understanding and does not provide clues about how to cope with the maternal relation *in the future*, how to exist in a milieu likely to contain an unusual concentration of persons in a similar (or worse) condition, and how eventually to 'pass that exam' to do the kind of job which would bring genuine interest. Laing partly mends this; it needs mending altogether.

Consider, too, one further point about the impact of Laingian ideas in the kind of milieu indicated of the loosely interlocking, partly employed, intellectually frustrated inhabitants of North London (and not only, of course, of North London). On the one hand, we have psychiatrists whom Laing rightly criticizes for opting out of the real task of analysis. On the other hand, we have 'patients' for whom the Laingian position comes as (literally) a godsend since they, defined as disturbed, are offered the counter-ideology of defining the world in general as mad. The world becomes defined as a malevolent Them with which no contact ought to be renewed and in which no job ought to be done. Thus unemployment and effortless sensitivity is ideologically legitimated. This separating out from the *body* of society, and the chronic fear of being reattracted to it by fiendish subtleties – this confused, bizarre denunciation of society – is the analogue of schizophrenia, at the social level. Laing essays to cure micro-schizophrenia by inducing macro-schizophrenia. He calls for responsibility by legitimating its opposite. There is nothing more seductive than to see oneself as a 'scapegoat' appointed by one's family and the system.

I have said that Laing is a preacher and that his congregation consists of the shaggy prophets of bed-sitterdom. As a preacher he is a heretic, and heresy means choice: he is in fact the apostle of spontaneous choice. His theology is obsessed with the secular loca-tion of original sin, tracing its taint from familial generation to generation. Unfortunately, like so many contemporary intel-lectuals, he believes in original sin *and* – when he permits himself some optimism – Rousseauesque means of social redemption. Now, a secular version of original sin makes the whole world mad by defining man himself as innocent. Like Jeff Nuttall,[4] another prophet in similar vein, he holds to the Augustinian and Rous-seauesque view at the same time and has the two in a state of mis-conceived relation. The great tradition of the church has been concerned to hold both original sin and the rational possibility open to man in creative relation. The rational possibility must not be denied, but it is made *impossible* if the fact of man's radical devia-tion from his centre is stood on its head. It is this radical deviation from his centre which not only 'infects' all structures but also creates that radical incongruity which is the key to all movement and dynamism.

Laing's fundamental error is that he wishes to cure the 'lack of fit' in human affairs and, therefore, attacks the common condition of man and the tragic comedy which legitimately belongs to it.

[4] See my comments on Nuttall's *Bomb Culture* (1969), in *Encounter*, August 1969.

9. The Image Breakers

The medium of television has been blamed for contributing to contemporary cultural dissolution both with regard to its characteristic mode *of presentation and the* content *it promotes. The mode is imagistic and kaleidoscopic, the content derived largely from the personalist philosophy of the intellectual fringe. Pictures cannot convey abstract arguments but they can suggest, and what they suggest is often dedicated to progressivist ideology, more especially in the fields of the arts and education. So far as education is concerned gimmicky experiments are susceptible to filming, sound learning is not. The experts employed are largely drawn from one viewpoint only and belong to that part of the academic world which shades ideologically and socially into the world of television. Indeed, television is a lodestar for the footloose graduate susceptible to the latest trend and also peculiarly antipathetic both to carefully sequential discussion on the one hand or to the business ethos on the other. The promotion of the left liberal consensus is justified as a necessary critique of 'the Establishment', a useful ploy which hides the established character of the opinions promoted. The primary technique is a juxtaposition between trendy expert and fruity reactionary. (Thus I was once asked to suggest some 'punitive personalities' who might represent old guard viewpoints.) The latter are presented as part of a Victorian syndrome to be contrasted tout court with the contemporary forces of light. The debate is conducted through crude contrasts and those who would like to have this or that specific element in the progressivist package are largely excluded. Their rhetorical difficulty derives from the fact that they have a position too complex for the medium and can be subjected to the contagious odium of association with Mrs. Whitehouse.*

'Television' writes T. C. Worsley in *Television: The Ephemeral*

Art, a collection of published programme reviews, 'is on the way towards re-uniting the imaginative world of the nation.' It mediates the collective self-image. But, he says, 'so radical has been the change in our status as a nation, that we have to set out all over again on the rediscovery of ourselves'. The problem involved in that change is not only the altered status of a nation but the confidence of a status group – the middle class – about propagating the image of 'culture' in the qualitative sense when it is guilty about its culture in the sociological sense.

Lord Reith and Britain's imperial position disappeared at about the same time. So the role that Mr. Worsley assigns to television is that of mediating the necessary changes in our sense of identity in a period when competition for mass audiences and the increased salience of alternative cultures, especially that of youth, have eroded the straight-forward educational tasks espoused in the early period of B.B.C. radio. The role is made more difficult because it is carried out by a medium whose images are extremely expendable. It drips steadily but cannot repeat. Its most obvious idols are adolescents on the verge of obsolescence. And the idol and image makers of the television world are often recruited from just those social milieux most dedicated to image breaking. In short, how do you negotiate the delicate transitions required to switch your national pantheon when some of the temple guardians are professional iconoclasts, not even assured of their own continuity and with reputations sometimes dependent on proclaimed and even demonstrated ability to break cherished conventions. Mr. Worsley has assigned the role of guardian to the evanescent practitioners of an 'ephemeral art'.

He poses the problems of this transition in terms of a conflict between an old middle class, using such damaged words as 'duty' and 'service' and now represented by Mrs. Whitehouse ('Queen Canute') and the newly enfranchised young who made it to the middle class through the channel of Redbrick. It is not easy to document the accuracy of this sociological observation, but it remains true that both the old and the new style are middle-class. One suspects that the more securely middle-class the young are the more iconoclastic their stance: but if one is uncertain about that particular piece of off-the-cuff sociology, one can definitely be sceptical about the suggestion that Mrs. Whitehouse and other protagonists of 'accepted standards' and the 'right-thinking majority' do not represent some very large battalions indeed. Nor of course is their habitat solely in that particular part of society which can be safely labelled funny and 'tasteless' because lower middle-class, and even funnier because its spokesman is a middle-aged woman. What is needed is to locate some of the elements in the consensus, whether right-thinking or not, and then estimate their social role, their likely staying power, their value. To some extent Mr. Worsley's stylish *obiter dicta* do make a beginning in this direction.

The first element of consensus is, paradoxically, that old middle-class attention to cultural standards. Not, of course, that the middle class *tout court* embodied these standards, but such standards were inevitably upheld by sections of the educated middle class. The paradox lies in the fact that these standards, though often ignored, except in the educationally aspiring segment of the respectable working class, were widely respected and still are, far more so than the trendy fashions of the contemporary 'new' middle class. If the standards were appropriated only by a minority, they were still very widely recognized. Just as some contemporary criminologists claim that criminals often recognize the moral code they break, so vast numbers of people accepted (and accept) cultural standards they ignore. Thus the B.B.C. in the days of Reith and Haley, was the repository of a national, as well as of a class, style. Moreover, whether it was middle-class or national, it was qualitatively very good indeed and not at all mealy-mouthed about its convictions: it recognized an élite of excellence and gave them a programme all of their own. It set out to educate.

The school which Reith and Haley created, and, in which many thousands were educated, is still there, even on television: those successors of the old Children's Hour 'Tom Tom' and 'Blue Peter', as well as 'Panorama', 'The Money Programme', 'Chronicle', 'Look Stranger', 'Master Class', and so on, B.B.C. news remains a stronghold of the Reith tradition: the impression of stringent objectivity, the disdain of sensationalism, and the establishmentarian accents of its announcers, conveying values by their very coolness, and by the tiniest inflections of tone, gesture and expression. It may be true that this particular audience has been augmented by what Mr. Worsley suggests could be an expanded B.B.C. 2 audience: a group not so cut off from the world of pop and sport, more interested in film, theatre and design and all things visual, less interested in books. But this new grouping need not do more than extend rather than replace the typical largesse of Auntie B.B.C. It is also true that the B.B.C. is seen by lower status groups as not 'ours' but 'theirs': but the alternative is simply that stream of mendacious advertisements, variety, crime films and Westerns represented by the commercial channels. The *popular* alternative to the old square B.B.C. is not the new trendies but Independent Television.

Some parts of that great, square, and (in the sense suggested) *national* tradition do not have to wilt under the changed external circumstances of Britain or the internal dynamics of the British status system. Those who implement the Reith tradition should not lose their nerve and forget the pupils he left behind. It contains features that our present circumstances could even reinforce. The old B.B.C. used to produce a programme, very properly around Sunday lunch time, which was a kind of anthology of 'rare-dear Britain': it was compounded of poems, intimations of bosky woods and banks, a background of Vaughan Williams and of larks ascending. That sense of one's own country is enormously important in any awareness of national identity, but it is supplemented by the specially English concern with archaeology, and now especially with industrial archaeology: the conservatism of a Constable extended by the industrial landscape of a Lowry, is something which can be cherished as unique to the world's first industrial nation. By programmes of this kind television still mediates our sense of being English. In another way Ealing Comedies did just this in the 1940s and 1950s.

But, equally, the sense of imperial destiny is doomed: the Trucial Scouts hardly feed a residual pride of empire. Just how difficult this transition may be is forgotten by those who were never paraded in the playground of a primary school to salute the flag on Empire Day. The same is true of the world role of Britain. Television news mediates and softens the slow transition to the status of a country that has (almost) no history. The superb B.B.C. television series of the Great War conveyed a sense of nostalgia which was more than balanced by a sense of the appalling cost of making and having history. Television processes world events for us within an acceptable frame, and however startling the events may be it familiarizes them acceptably.

But then there are the more problematic elements, neither so nostalgically necessary as our sense of 'England' nor so obviously doomed as imperial sentiment. These might be called the 'Big Ben' aspects of English culture. In the Newnes *Pictorial Knowledge*, issued some thirty or more years ago, there was a picture of the Palace of Westminster called 'The Mother of Parliaments'. The sense of pride in British democracy and institutions, and maybe also respect for the politicians who embody those institutions, is a point of strain and transition, and one which the fashionable accentuate by the images they project, or rather fail to project. In his Granada lecture, Mr. Richard Crossman referred to the trivialization of political debate by the media. Mr. Worsley denies that this trivialization is intentional on the part of the mediators, but he admits they may be party to the 'cheap popular prejudice that they (politicians) are all twisters, hypocrites and liars'.

Worse than that (which is disservice enough to the cause of democracy), it has been suggested, on credible authority, that the serious issues of the 1970 general election were deliberately scanted by television. The senior officials believed Harold Wilson would win anyway, and were unwilling to stir things up, while the left-wing producers considered the whole electoral process as no more than an insignificant farce. The persistent recruitment of young sophisticates with this view of parliamentary democracy is serious. It is not confined to Britain, but is, for example, the subject of concerned comment in Sweden, while Italian television, too, is largely controlled by the extreme Left.

This orientation of young recruits is much less evident in overt news than in the images projected of different segments of our social structure. The images of the commercial middle class on the

media appear to concentrate wonderfully on a subliminal denigra-
tion of their characteristic psychology. (Or why not include the
arrogant professions of doctors in the critical catalogue?) With the
possible exception of 'Mogul' one hardly ever sees a sympathetic
portrayal of a business-man. Take the values underlying a recent
interesting television series called 'The Family of Man'. There,
families in Esher were subjected to a commentary which precisely
echoed current prejudices against suburbia: the fact that the inhabitants of Esher played into the hands of their mocking television
observers and interlocutors is irrelevant. One collected the strong
impression that the only 'genuine' or 'real' people were those in
Nelson and Colne, or even better, those in New Guinea. A recent
letter in the *Radio Times* neatly caught this undercurrent of suggestion: 'This reference to "real people" and "real marriages" – what
other kinds are there? . . . I have often been puzzled by this
strange, modern belief that only dwellers in council houses are
"real".'

Another traditional part of the national consensus is religion.
This does not mean that many people want to watch church
services, or even that they are so very interested in discussion programmes, but there is a diffuse respect for the notion of religion
and even to a lesser degree for the Church. Those who share in this
diffuse respect may or may not watch programmes like 'Meeting
Point'. If they do they must have the impression that one of its
principal aims is to vent the opinions of a group of clergy com-
muting between London and Cambridge, whose difficulties are
nothing if not peculiarly their own. No doubt this is a continuous
problem for television, which is accentuated when it deals with
religion; the need to ignore ongoing continuities and permanent
symbols in the search for what's new, Malcolm Muggeridge is, of
course, an adept performer and Mr. Worsley rightly characterizes
him as the kind of lashing critic of our morals who enunciates our
uncertainties just enough to allow us to go on as before. Muggeridge's method is a simple juxtaposition of the Gospels with political
reality which creates a glaring contrast without any illumination of
either. Politics and politicians are once again handed over to the
realm of darkness and the level of political discussion associated

with these juxtapositions is totally devoid of any of the relevant moral and empirical complexity.

In this, of course, Mr. Muggeridge is no worse than the other ringmasters of debate. All too frequently one has a man presiding over an issue who does not understand the structure of the argument or its necessary development, but is concerned only to juxtapose naked attitudinizing. Maybe this exhibition of antagonistic postures is inherent in the medium, but it is none the less objectionable and contributes to the trivialization of debate. Even on documentaries the search for the startling or merely curious view can result in very serious distortion of the weight of expert opinion. A recent B.B.C. programme on population consisted of facts which were 50 per cent inaccurate combined with varieties of simplistic inference which were nearly 100 per cent illegitimate. There was not a single demographer on the programme. It had obviously not occurred to the producers that this was not merely an occasion for exploring startling opinions, but an immensely complicated matter of social scientific *fact*.

Perhaps the actual state of debate is no worse than it ever was, but television must be contributing to an increasing illusion of actually knowing something about these matters.

One can't help wondering, when viewing such programmes, whether McLuhanite suppositions do not have some substance. Mr. Worsley speaks of a growing audience of people who are sensitive but do not read books. That is a polite way of referring to factual ignorance and it is curiously analogous to the condition of some contemporary students, presumably brought up under the combined impact of modern educational theory and television. One would like to inquire whether their disdain for fact, dislike of books, tiny time-span of attention and incapacity for extended discursive thought have anything to do with being massaged by the medium. Both the extended logic of an A. J. Ayer and the extended rhetoric of (say) a George Brown, seem to be unavailable to them. For such, there are not only certain damaged words – 'reason', 'fact', and 'science', as well as 'wholesome', 'decent', 'service' and 'duty' – but words as such are damaged. Reactions are sacred, facts are free.

A central element of consensus in Britain is our attitude to law and order. The soporific benevolence of 'Dixon of Dock Green' has progressed to the realpolitik of Barlow, but it is still only the trendier section of the middle class, and the underworld it professes to admire, who call the police 'the fuzz'. 'In a violent society, and with widely differing standards', said a recent documentary, 'how long can The Jolly Copper go on marching?' But as a matter of fact we are not a violent society. That much becomes clear in turning to J. D. Halloran, R. L. Brown and D. C. Chaney on *Television and Delinquency*. They begin by defining the problem not primarily as a matter of increasing violence but as a matter of perceived threat to cherished values and a demand for remedial action. They do not deny the extent of the feeling that Mrs. Whitehouse represents, indeed they point out that a 'refusal to accept the values of the so-called permissive society, may be more widespread than many people think', but the identification of television as the locus both of cause and, therefore, of remedy, is defined as the attitude of those seeking rapid answers. In any case, as Mr. Worsley points out, these people generally ignore the violence of the I.T.V. routine thriller to concentrate on the more biting violence exhibited by ciné-vérité techniques.

There *is* a disproportionate rise in crimes against the person and an increase in delinquency in the 15–20 years age range, but traffic offences are after all much the most frequent type of case, with offences against property following: violence accounted for 2 per cent of all people found guilty of offences in 1968. By delinquency we mean theft. In summarizing the literature on this subject Messrs. Halloran, Brown and Chaney suggest that the media are of only marginal importance, triggers at the most, and that direct experiences are far more crucial than vicarious ones. It is difficult to do justice to the cool objectivity of this discussion: its sensitive handling of the distortions and difficulties of criminal statistics, its indication of the complicated web of causality, of the variety of possible approaches and distinct levels of theoretical concern, of the question of the broader social context and the inevitable cost of a given type of social organization. They cite work indicating that criminals evade the morality of society rather than denying it;

their values and beliefs are 'essentially conservative' and broadly similar to the rest of the *lower* working class. Once again the consensual element in our society is brought out.

The authors' own study, reported in their book, seems to bear these contentions out: the probationers they examined used the media in terms of a pattern of lower-working-class culture. This involved an emphasis on immediacy of emotional impact and emotional gratification, cognitive and logical poverty, undeveloped social skills, emphasis on masculinity and on male company, and fantasy seeking. All this occurred in the context of families where the father is semi-skilled, or there is a missing parent, or many siblings, or inadequate attention, or haphazard discipline and poor management, or any combination of these things. These factors contributed to their delinquency *and* to their viewing preferences. Their delinquency and their television viewing were an integral part of their overall pattern of leisure.

The gist of all this is that there *are* strains in what sociologists call our central value system. The contrasting generations in both the Garnett and the Steptoe families neatly focus that strain, and, like the other great comedy programmes – Peter Cook and Dudley Moore, Alan Bennett, Monty Python – their satirical targets include trends as well as traditions. But there are two separate battles, which do not gain by being confused. There is the campaign centred in Mrs. Whitehouse which is largely dedicated to cosiness, and which is also compromised both by its vocabulary and by the other causes too frequently associated with it. Its propagandists make the rhetorical blunder of defending 'law and order' when they should lament the unpleasantness of good working-class policemen having to put up with insult and insurrection from the spoilt children of the middle class. 'Decency' suffers if it can be arguably linked to the return of capital punishment and brutality towards homosexuals. The other campaign is to retain those great, square commitments of the old B.B.C. and the values of a logical, factual, complex, extended verbal culture against every form of triviality, against anarchic subjectivism, and against a dominant concern with the ethnography of attitude. It is a battle joined not only in television and radio, but within several great newspapers, the universities and the Church.

Symbols convey identity and continuity and our society has achieved its high degree of peace and order by an unusual reliance on arbitrary symbols as compared to rational legitimation. This forces it to be implicit in its expression and to avoid that explicit use of force which a more rational system would have the unhappy confidence to employ. In short, it is a highly Oakeshottian society based on ways of acting and feeling. Thus, even the straightforward defence of excellence is inhibited, while the critics are able to extend the instant rhetoric of equality and self-expression without regard to particular contexts. English society is highly particularistic and thereby protects individuality. To be variegated is not to be fundamentally divided; quite the reverse. Our symbols are our dreams about ourselves and maybe the guardians of our collective image should be careful how they tread on our dreams. Professor Mary Douglas has argued that the dislocation of arbitrary symbols (fish on Fridays) can unhinge whole ranges of metaphysic and assumptions about acceptable conduct. The evidence is not yet in, but one hopes the guardians of our temples know what they are about.

10.   The Art of Persuasion

The 'Oz' case provided the cause celèbre of mid-1971. The case was interesting not merely as an example of misplaced zeal on the part of the authorities but because it encouraged a display of progressive rhetoric on a large-scale. This rhetorical style, based primarily on variants of the 'tu quoque' ploy was extremely popular with media men and the 'Guardian' sector of the intellectual and pseudo-intellectual middle class. As a style of argument it deserves prolonged analysis, and this short piece is designed only to indicate a few of the methods employed, mostly through letters to the Press. As a rhetorical style it was and is very effective and many people opposed to this or that element in the progressive 'package' find themselves harried and silenced by its use. The most pervasive element is a bastard mutation of the Christian doctrine of martyrdom transferred to whoever breaks current norms of decency. The 'martyr' cum artist-innovator is the first ripple of the future and few dare stand out against the incoming tide. Thus any folly and indecency can be legitimated, provided enough conventional people can be persuaded to object to it. Once the conventional can be claimed as opponents no progressive dare be caught in a critical stance. In any case, how can apostles of the naked soul and the naked body be accused of 'having no clothes'?

The 'Oz' case has by now lost most of its interest for the media and all that can remain is to observe the controversy itself. Such a furious verbal confrontation retains an interest as a striking focus of the contemporary rhetoric of persuasion, particularly as exercised in the minor art of writing to the newspapers.

By rhetoric I mean the artful argumentum ad hominem exemplified in the basic ploys of verbal encounter. The rules of this art are relatively unformalized as compared with systematic logic since the aim is less to be right than to be seen to be right. Triumph matters more than rectitude. The writer partly seeks to persuade, partly to indicate the volume of those who are of his persuasion, partly to exhibit publicly his own right attitudes to what ever is his reference group. Clearly the rules of such an exercise are likely to be localized: as Pascal observed of jurisprudence it is liable to differ with 1° of latitude.

The 'Oz' controversy illustrates contemporary rhetoric so well, not only because it trespasses on jurisprudence, but because it vaguely invokes the social sciences and assumptions about the human norm and acceptable or at any rate tolerable divergences from it. Whereas more directly political exchanges have often involved rhetorical competition over being more genuinely proletarian the 'Oz' controversy activates rival claims to being more genuinely human.

The manner in which one suggests one's breadth of humanity, the depth of one's existential concern and one's sense of humane priorities is the key to controversial supremacy. The favourable presentation of the self is achieved by one's commendatory vocabulary: one admires and therefore by implication exemplifies frankness, openness, creativity, innovation, compassion, lack of hypocrisy. The humanity of one's opponents is best undermined by a sadly objective 'analysis' of their psychological condition. Moral repulsion dressed up in psychiatric terminology is always preferable to the straight-forward language of outraged morals and enables the clever to triumph over the conventionally good by the nimble use of 'pathological', 'paranoid' or 'hysterical'. 'Authoritarian' still retains its abusive impact because it indicates a specific social attitude linked to a diagnosable psychological condition and further linked to Right-wing politics. And it is infinitely transferable without much regard to context. 'Repulsive' or 'disgusting' are very ineffective by comparison and 'sick minds' lacks the clinical overtone. To accuse people of 'beastliness' or 'bestiality' only succeeds in suggesting a lack of rich, vital energy in oneself, a deficiency of animal spirits. 'Wicked' is, of course, based so clearly on notions of good and evil as to cut no ice whatsoever.

The extent to which psychiatry provides the vocabulary of abuse is indicated by the fact that the basic 'tu quoque' argument takes a psychiatric form: for example, the more you protest the more infected you are by the repression of that condition against which you are protesting. The older moralistic variant of tu quoque depended on the assertion that the opponent had gone and done likewise; the psychological cum-progressivist version depends on the reverse assertion, that the opponent has exercised a pathological degree of control in failing to do so. Surprisingly enough both forms of tu quoque are often used together.

Tu quoque has its uses outside the psychiatric ambience. Its optimum employment is achieved by taking the opponents' preferred abusive epithet and re-applying it to another moral context in which he can be more plausibly implicated. Thus the term 'obscene' used with respect to sexuality needs to be hurled back attached to war, slums, unemployment, or the social system in general, responsibility for which should be placed at the door of the opposition. The most original use of this technique in the 'Oz' controversy firmly attached 'obscene' to the fees of the barristers involved.

Another neat transfer is based on the technique developed in pub controversy over religion which asserts 'The Bible is a dirty book; I wouldn't let my daughter read it'. This moral sensitivity could be deployed against the newspapers favourable to the trial. Thus The Times and the Daily Telegraph became 'obscene', a charge referring to content but occasionally documented by citation of issues containing nude photographs. The most economical use of this technique begins 'Hiding my Times behind my copy of "Oz" . . .' One then goes on to say that obscenity is in the eye of the beholder.

Transferred epithets are part of the wider moral contest (or mote and beam) type of argument based on the discernment of greater moral evils which either dwarf the supposed evil under discussion, or, better still, are responsible for it. Thus the mote and beam argument becomes linked to the powerful rhetorical technique based on 'symptom not cause' that is, not only is the evil currently raged against small but it is a mere symptom of the greater evil. For example, it is important to suggest that pornography is merely an inevitable and morally irrelevant consequence of 'the system'. Though the argument that X is a relatively small evil can be rebutted by suggesting that it does not become justified by the existence of greater evil Y the suggestion that X is symptom of Y is irrefutable. It can only be met by reversing the causal sequence that is by claiming that obscenity gives rise to homelessness which gives rise to war. The best form of 'symptom not cause' suggests that there is a single cause (that is guilt) responsible both for all the acknowledged greater evils *and* your opponents objections to the smaller evil.

A minor variant on the 'who hath the greater evil' contest is based on reference to 'the hitherto neglected aspect'. Letters of this kind begin 'A great deal of attention seems to have been given to such and such aspect of the issue, but what really appals and depresses me is so and so . . .' This neglected aspect need not be a greater evil but it is greater in that it has been so much overlooked by the embattled and the impercipient. It also facilitates the entry of hobby horses as, for example, the architect who managed to sneak in a quick one against other architects by claiming that pornography was only necessary because they had made such a mess of our town centres.

One further twist and this becomes the very effective approach based on the claim to a cross-bench position, for example 'I am over 40 but I humbly wish to learn from the younger generation'. Since independent views are widely believed to be more genuinely formed than those of mere party hacks, it is important to acquire a cross-bench position, especially if you can claim that normally you are associated with one side but in this instance line up with the other. Thus 'I am not and never have been a member of the demi-monde but . . .' is moderately effective yet lacks bite compared with 'As a member of the National Council for Civil Liberties I favour any censorship which protects children from racism or pornography'. Here the technique of the greater evil (racism) is effectively countered by a blanket linkage of both evils under the rubric of the protection of children (and if children are being protected from capitalist exploitation so much the better).

Much rhetoric employs the 'As an X' approach, asserting a relevant role, interest or expertise. Relevant roles are exemplified in 'As a parent' and 'As a father of young children' and can be extended towards socially useful occupations such as teachers and probation officers (people rarely write 'as' brewers, capitalists or pornographers). Relevant expertise is more frequently indicated by title or institution at the foot of a letter. This usually involves reference to official Reports or to 'the Danish experience' or 'studies'. Should expert opinion appear to waver one need do no more than assert, as did one psychiatrist, that all *informed* opinion' sided with him. 'Studies' are made more impressive by technical references (matched controls, chi-square) and require very little direct linkage to the actual topic under discussion beyond the bland assertion that 'Recent research has conclusively shown'. This counters the older assertion that 'all history proves' (especially of course the history of the decline and fall of the Roman Empire).

Apart from the decline of Rome, which attracts by virtue of the very large number of possible reasons which can be adduced for it, compelling historical instances are few and stereotyped. Broadly the only other examples are early Christians, early socialists, one (fairly) early Greek – Socrates, and one Renaissance man – Galileo. Socrates appears on both sides, either complaining about youthful degeneration or as murdered by 'the Establishment'. (Reference to 'the Establishment' as the enemies of those whom one supports are, of course, de rigueur.) Any group under attack can be assimilated to the early Christians, unless one happens to believe the early Christians were responsible for the decline and fall of the Roman Empire. Early Socialists were neatly deployed by the *Daily Telegraph* on the ground that they had not created the Labour Movement merely to make Britain fit for pornographers. Early socialists (good) are not to be compared with late Victorians (bad) or Puritans (very bad) in spite of being both. Those ancient figures of rhetoric, the Victorians and Puritans, are still in use by the libertarian left in spite of the fact that Puritans conducted the only successful revolution in these islands.

Most historical references attempt to attach the contagious odium of Hitler or the Soviet Union to one's opponent. Thus one correspondent achieved this by claiming that the *Daily Telegraph* failed to attack the alternative society represented by Hitler in 1933 while another claimed that any attempt at censorship was 'reminiscent' of the methods of the Soviet Union. A neat counter from the liberal Right suggests that libertarian phenomena of this type immediately preceded Hitler, thereby effectively spreading contagious odium backwards.

Proponents of counter-cultures or alternative life styles (sociological terms are increasingly used in debate) normally defend the rights of minorities but there is also recourse to the theme of the significant and misunderstood pioneer which suggests that though innovators always have to face martyrdom their ideas are triumphing with the new generation. Few people like to be explicitly against the evolutionary tide: 'I may be old fashioned but . . .' is the nearest to a stand against Evolution and History. Those who feel they are being threatened by social evolution normally have recourse not to counter-evolution but to democracy as the best riposte. They are sure that 90 per cent of the people of this country agree with them, as against the noisy, the vociferous, the vocal 10 per cent. Like Chesterton they call on the silent majority. 'The people of England they have not spoken yet'. This approach can be illustrated by appropriate moral exemplars amongst whom clean-limbed runners or unaccompanied yachtsmen (Chay Blyth, Francis Chichester) are well to the fore. Part of the minority response against the majority (or the Establishment) involves a rhetoric of butterflies broken on wheels, caterpillars crushed by sledgehammers. For obvious reasons in the 'Oz' case no sledgehammers were used against nuts. One clergyman carried the pathos of this approach to a high level by commenting that a frightened Establishment was trying to crush 'an alternative form of blessedness'.

An instructive paradigm of many of the attitudes and techniques of deciding approval or disapproval was provided at the same time as the 'Oz' affair by the Snow incident. In this case Snow offended against several criteria of approval: he jostled a *small coloured* man in a game of cricket. This looked as if Snow might be labelled both a racist and a bully, but several points appeared in his favour. First he was condemned by 'the Establishment' which suggested extenuating circumstances. Second, Cricket is intrinsically a rather prissy Establishmentariam affair and he was only bringing to the game a natural boisterousness and vigour which would have been perfectly acceptable in a less class-ridden game like football. Third, his father was a clergyman and he had attended a public school, so he was naturally hardly culpable at all because a background of the ten commandments and good manners could only lead to a wholly understandable dislike of all regulations. *Ergo*, he was an innocent victim of 'the system'.

Moral: innocence is a function of the existence of the Establishment. Abolish the Establishment and dissent might easily become culpable. The innocence and legitimation of our dissenters depends too directly and obviously on the existence of our Establishment to make them seriously wish to destroy it.

NOTE:

I have omitted one major technique in my discussion. This is a reference back to an accepted reform in the past, followed up by the contention that the argument for the present 'reform' has exactly the same logical status as that for the previous one, and has in some unspecified way an evolutionary continuity with it. It is essential to use the word 'reform' about any proposal, especially if one's purpose is (to use the favourite counter-phrase) 'to turn the clock back'. It is always advisable for progressives to use the phrase 'dragged kicking and screaming into the twentieth century'.

For an excellent discussion of the abusive potential and covert moral use of psychiatric terms cf. Rupert Wilkinson *The Broken Rebel. A Study in Culture, Politics and Authoritarian Character* (1973). His remarks on the use of 'sick', on how to give the clinical tone to a dogmatic cynicism, and how to 'pathologize' one's opponents are very well taken.

11. Black Papers and White Immigrants

The institutional area most affected by psychic subversion and the ideology of the experiencing subject is the School. Many teachers were affected by this ideology as it dribbled downward, even though its original provenance in the liberal upper middle class was far removed from their own social location. Even those teachers with a preference for skills, mastery and disciplined effort lacked a rhetoric to utilize against the proponents of self-expression. They could only murmur 'I suppose I'm too old-fashioned, but . . .' The effect was to weaken the effort to pass on basic skills and this had a most deleterious impact on the intellectual potential of those from less privileged backgrounds. The contempt for logic and structure was unfortunate even in middle class sectors but it was less disabling than the loss of basic skills sustained by the working class. Curiously enough this permeation of an upper middle class ideology was supported by the contention that the working class had no right to the wealth of civilization because hitherto it had been so largely monopolized by upper status groups. Progressives wavered between regarding working class people as deprived and as possessing a culture too marvellous to be tampered with. This review of the Black Papers reflects a critical sympathy with their efforts to stem the tide of fashion. The issue was not comprehensivization: it was whether or not learning is osmotic or structured. The second section of the review is largely concerned with rebutting what was a popular thesis of 'The New Left': the idea that England was so much a stagnant pool that even its conservatism needed to be expressed by 'white' (right wing) immigrants.

The two 'Black Paper' collections of short pieces by Cox and Dyson[1] are addressed to influential people in order to help save the

[1] *Fight for Education*, Two Black Papers, Edited by C. B. Cox and A. E. Dyson, Critical Quarterly Society.

traditional notion of education; '*Student Power*'[2] is about the redemption of thought and how to disrupt the citadels of false consciousness in the University. There is therefore some disparity of aim as well as of politics. In the former case it is not always easy to see the criteria of inclusion, except that they all connect with the heading of the Introduction to Black Paper No. 1 'Progressive Collapse'. In the latter case the criteria are clear: everything is connected to everything else so nothing is really irrelevant. Colonialism, linguistic philosophy, war, bureaucracy, schizophrenia, boredom – all are due to capitalism.

The aims of Black Paper No. 1 are as follows. We must maintain standards, accept intellectual discipline, and refuse to pander to the wayward arrogance of a pampered youth. A University exists to do research and to transmit knowledge; a school is a place of learning rather than a temple of self-expression. Current troubles can only lead in the end to more state intervention in universities, police maybe, and certainly ignorant intruders like the Prices & Income Board brandishing their irrelevant yardsticks of 'productivity'. Intellectual excellence and self-discipline are assisted by examinations which are, after all, partly tests of professional competence. If students like desultory reading or want communitarian therapy and/or revolutionary activism then they are entitled to have them, but such things do not require universities or public money. Nor do universities require the presence of that celebrated non-subject sociology – which Robert Conquest oddly likens to courses in water-skiing at the University of Florida.

Conquest's remark does suggest the merits and demerits of the *Black Paper*. It is, for instance, occasionally funny, which can hardly be said of its red rival. Conquest also reminds us that the clash of 'repressed' youth with 'those beetle-browed thugs Professor X and Mr Y' is a richly comic invention. (As one Student Leader put it to me: 'The trouble is there is *no* authority around here – the place is dying of democracy gone mad'). The *Black Paper* is also commendably resolute in rejecting those vague sentimentalities supposedly validated by research, or by the practices of some populist institution in Minnesota which form the pabulum of forward

[2] *Student Power*, Edited by A. Cockburn and R. Blackburn, Penguin.

educational thinking. It even dares use words like 'immaturity' and 'cheating' without embarrassment. Whatever next? (We'll be referring to student pamphlets as 'lies' before long.) But it has no context, in short, almost no 'sociology'. It describes without analysing the social background, and shows irritation without wider understanding. Bryan Wilson's article is the main exception. His arguments will madden all those who think sociology must show the folly or irrelevance of traditional values and confirm all those who regard it as a tattered cloak thrown over bourgeois interests. Bryan Wilson points to generation conflict rather than to class conflict, to the prejudice against age and the disdain of seniority, to the spread of 'the fun ethic' and 'entertainment values'. For him the dislocations of expansion have weakened the capacity of tradition to reproduce itself, either amongst students or amongst some younger academics. The values of productivity have partly eroded those criteria of intellectual enrichment which might more easily and properly have evoked their loyalty. Furthermore, the intimate social contours of college life have become large grey unknowns in which suspicion runs riot. And behind the banners and the idealism 'lurks self-interest and wounded hopes' as well as the search for meaning and identity.

Unfortunately, there is much to be said for this approach. Anyone who has discussed for as long as I have with revolutionary students must be aware that their large ideological talk serves as a convenient excuse for rudeness, as a pretext for arrogant posturing and as a licence for intermittent carnival, plus the added bonus of exposure in the mass media. Bryan Wilson's refusal to accept the banners at their face value (who said sociology only goes for the appearance?) directs our attention to the sheer petulant fractiousness behind the bulk of their day-to-day clamour. The complaints about the Universe and about the Coffee-machine, and the technique of wearing out liberals by playing on the weak structure of authority and on donnish scruples is reminiscent of the tactics of the spoilt child. He makes everybody's life a burden, works the system entirely for his own convenience, and then claims he is the Victim. As one militant sympathizer at last confessed: 'They are insatiable . . .'

In the second *Black Paper* the broad attacks of the first are documented and the universities are relegated to a more subordinate role. The argument turns partly on the preservation of the grammar schools and partly on the use of 'progressive' (or 'discovery') methods.

Reading the paper and its counter-blast 'Verdict on the Facts' (edited by Brian Jackson and Beryl McAthlone for Advisory Council for Education) one can't help but be disquieted at the extent to which one is offered a package deal by both sides of the debate. What can anyone say who is cautiously in favour of comprehensive schools and who applauds certain types of progressive method provided they do not exclude the necessary formal elements? Curiously enough the *Black Paper* would offer such a person a wider range of option than the Advisory Council for Education pamphlet, which presents a characteristic syndrome of opinion offered for general acceptance without admitting that one may dislike selection at 11, suspect certain elements in the instructional methods of the grammar schools, yet also wish to distinguish carefully between a legitimate authority (which guides and supports) and mere authoritarianism, and generally desire to assess each area of concern independently. That, at least, is my own position. So far as examinations go I want some relatively objective test, which is why I am against continuous assessment by teachers; I do not want to replace the occasional examination by continuous appraisal with an increased subjective component. So far as methods are at issue I would want to see how they work out in various contexts. As June Wedgewood Benn points out in the *Black Paper*, we must separate the issues of methods, of higher education and student unrest, and of 'going comprehensive'. There is also the explosive issue of moral education (which the *Black Paper* editors wisely skirt) and the complicated matter of teacher training, not to mention the crucial questions of teachers' morale and competence in non-teaching skills. Far too little attention has been given to training for the special *administrative* problems of comprehensives, to their need of 'cabinet government', and to the criteria of selection for senior posts.

Much of what I would wish to say relates to this question of

morale, since it is distinctly my impression that morale is sometimes low, and where this is so progressive methods are a useful
smokescreen to mislead anxious parents. The parent who looks at
his children's books and is fascinated by the unruly rubbish therein
is told he was brought up in the 'dark ages' of education and cannot
hope to penetrate the creative excitement which lies behind the
apparently footling inadequacies of the actual work (even though
the creative excitement has not been quite enough to persuade his
teacher to look at it). But more of that below: both *Black Paper* and
the Advisory Council for Education pamphlet are partly anecdotal
and I perforce must be the same: although my experience is simply
that of a trained primary school teacher, a university teacher, and
a parent.

I should say straight away that, having taught children myself, I
by no means feel in a position to criticize school teachers un-
reservedly. It is an extraordinarily exacting profession and one
which I left without a sigh. Unfortunately it is the one profession
where competence in the *teaching* aspect – except at the margin – is
not acquired by instruction. Teaching cannot be taught, and my
experience of a college of education was that they did not waste
too much time trying. Teaching provides the prime instance of the
discovery method, of knowledge by experience, and the experience is often rather painful, partly because a fair number of
teachers go into the schools not out of talent or commitment but
faute de mieux. It is the uncomfortable but least bothersome refuge
of many an amiable drone. For such the mystique of progressive
flexibility is a linguistic camouflage for careless disorganization. Of
course if progressive methods can be shown to work only with the
best teachers, and if comprehensive modes of organization positively encourage disintegrating morale, then a wider range of
doubt is involved than simply the condition of the teaching profession. Certainly comprehensives sometimes lack the *esprit de
corps* (even, on occasion, the self-respect) of the grammar school,
but on the whole I'm inclined to put a fair amount down to the
pangs of transition. How the variable impact of all the different
factors involved can be summed up is, in any case, beyond my
comprehension. One uses one's information largely to back one's

hunches and one's prejudices. To be sure, both sides claim 'research' is on *their* side. But as a practising sociologist I can only say that in very little research do the facts unambiguously imply what they are supposed to imply. They may mean this or that according to how you interpret adventitious factors in a much wider context than that actually under review. In the past, fools supported their opinions by the assertion 'all history shows –'; nowadays as we have noted earlier, fools document their prejudices with the assertion 'recent research conclusively proves . . .'

Research is, all the same, preferable to anecdotes, but anecdotes can sometimes illustrate a point, and the curious tale of my own son's education provides me with ammunition to suspect both selection at 11 and certain aspects of progressive methods. Local and unrepresentative it may be but I meet too many parents with identical experiences to suppose it is entirely peculiar to the area in which I happen to live. Indeed the writers of the Advisory Council for Education pamphlet admit widespread disquiet, though they call it 'bewilderment', in order to suggest that it is largely due to lack of information. Some of us are not so uninformed as the patronizing tone of the enlightened would suggest.

Unlike the children of so many of my progressive friends, my son actually goes to a state comprehensive school, and a short while ago I had the interesting experience of having to look after his education personally while abroad. The school very kindly provided me with the necessary textbooks – in those areas where 'texts' still existed – and I set about the task (I may say in parenthesis that this was a good school, not neglecting its lower ability pupils in order to ape the grammar school, and maintaining a very good Sixth Form even though deprived of 'the cream').

The new Nuffield Mathematics appealed to me as immensely superior to the mathematics I failed to learn at my own school. What I did discover, however, was that my son, at thirteen, knew almost no basic computational skills (that is simple division) or the difference between a fraction and a decimal. This was partly an indictment of his primary school, but it also seemed his present teachers were not aware of this lack, or had not thought it worth-while apprising me of it. In French I already knew that after six months regular teaching, he had heard neither of *avoir* nor *être*, let alone, of course, the notion of an infinitive. He had acquired at that time – or later – no transferable skills, no sense of that structure around which knowledge can be built, and at times he did not even recognize a written word simply because it was known only in the context of the language laboratory. In short, far from initiating him into *principles* (such as was clearly the object of the Nuffield Mathematics) he had a phrase-book knowledge, woodenly applic-able only in the most limited contexts. At the time when it became necessary for me to teach him, progress was still so slow that no sense of cumulative achievement was possible, let alone any aware-ness of a cumulative hierarchy of skills. Yet by giving him only the normal quota of French lessons (admittedly on a personal basis) and initiating him into the pleasures of problem-solving through the application of rules, he was reading fourth-year grammar-school texts with ease in the course of fourteen weeks. Understanding had replaced free association.

This narration has a simple but crucial point: progressive methods are more developed, or work better, in some contexts than others, and should rarely be relied on to the exclusion of formal teaching. And this is what Professor Bantock, in the most distinguished essay in the *Black Paper*, says: 'Used competently these new methods have a great deal to offer. Used incompetently . . . they are probably more disastrous to learning than reliance on the old formal methods'. If united to a philosophy of educational *laisser faire* (or mere laziness) and to the setting of homework so infrequently and unsystematically as to arouse resentment that any should have been set at all, they are clearly a passport to effortless inferiority. Yet this does *not* mean we need return to the routine of mere note-taking or the rigidities and compartmentalism of many traditional grammar schools. Those institutions no more produced people who could *think* (as distinct from executing exercises through conventional intellectual hoops) than does an exclusive concentration on 'the play way'.

This is what some of the *Black Paper* contributors ignore, and it connects unhappily with their dislike of sociology (not to mention their egregious ignorance of it). Oddly enough sociology is what happens when you stop *learning* history or *acquiring* moral rules and start to think about both. That a great number of people do it in an immature way is not surprising; after all, a great deal of what passes for history is bunk too. Sociology, like history, contains such a great deal of bunk not because it is easy but because it is difficult and involves thinking, an activity which neither the more traditionally minded grammar school nor the bogus progressives sold on 'creativity' have much interest. For the former it would open the door to general ideas; for the latter it would put logic and order into the operations of the vagrant imagination.

We need to ask why it is that bogus progressives achieve such éclat in our contemporary society. What is the power of O.K. thinking? It is not a question to be answered in a paragraph. Partly, of course, there is the itch to crackpot activism: If something is in actual operation and even working, it is high time to change it. Partly there is the impact of what can only be called 'Sneer and Smear Cultures' (to contrast with what Professor Baroja called 'Honour and Shame Cultures'). In parts of the progressive middle class, sneering has gone beyond a technique employed occasionally in self-defence and has become a way of life. Increasingly it is supplemented by the smear, which has been brought to a remarkable degree of obscene refinement by young idealists in our universities. Anyone who disagrees at any point with this prescribed syndrome of O.K. opinion (who, in short, wants to think independently) is labelled as part of 'the backlash', or, to take my own case, as a 'fascist-liberal'. (Amis and Conquest describe how one critic actually went so far as to call them – Christians!) As for the O.K. militant, he fears nothing more than a wrong label on himself: it might push him out into a wilderness of real social heresies as distinct from the comfortable conformity of the radical hive. It is this warm buzz of progressive complacency which gives rise to what Edward Boyle wittily describes as an 'ugly backlash from moderate, unfanatical, middle-of-the-road opinion'.

Where is this 'backlash' of the moderate, tolerant, middle-of-the-roader to be socially located? Partly it is among those scholarship boys who identify with a system which was so perspicacious as to choose *them*. They suspect that the standards of excellence which they first encountered through the grammar school will no longer hold once its institutional frame is destroyed. They also suspect (with far more reason) that the Labour Party will destroy the institutions of the bright upper working-class and the solid middle citizenry while leaving alone the schools of the very rich (after all, it may be argued, Eton has gone comprehensive already). In this last suspicion I fear they may be right.

In commenting above on the first *Black Paper* I referred to the tactics of the spoilt child so popular among students. *Student Power* recognizes that it is faced with a problem in mobilizing this infantilism into a coherent force: somehow one needs to throw a Marxist cloak over what is, in part, a generational gripe. The advantage of such a cloak is that it has been woven without seam throughout so that all the ills of mankind are brought to the door of Capitalism and Bureaucracy. *An alert student leadership can show the concealed systematic relationship between sexual controls, university authoritarianism, economic exploitation and imperialist aggression.* Determined revolutionaries are themselves aware that however easy it may be to play on vague suspicions and half-informed disgruntlement, it is less easy to build so evanescent a phase into a disciplined revolutionary thrust, unless other co-operating factors are present. Hence the inevitable references in some articles to the need to awake the Sleeping Beauty of the English working class.

However, most of the book is about the University. Carl Davidson is required reading for the techniques of destroying the major educational institutions of the West *by avoiding compromise and reform*. Tom Fawthrop's piece on examinations is worth reading in conjunction with C. B. Cox's 'In Praise of Examinations' in the *Black Paper*.[3] Triesman exhibits shock and contempt over the

[3] On p. 324 Halliday seems to approve the following useful idea from China's cultural revolution: students set their own examinations with the approval of

activities of the C.I.A.; Fred Halliday provides an overall view of international student activity; Linda Tinkham writes sensibly about 'the women's place' in colleges of education, while Tom Nairn and Jim Singh-Sadhu provide an illuminating survey of the art college situation. David Adelstein runs through familiar material on inequalities in the educational system, dilates on the iniquity of the binary system, and ends with a demand for consumer power: the transient consumers of the university 'product' should capitalize on adolescent inexperience to control the permanent life situation of those who have made scholarship a vocation (he doesn't put it *quite* like that).[4]

Perhaps the two most interesting essays are Robin Blackburn's 'Brief Guide to Bourgeois Ideology' and Perry Anderson's 'Components of the National Culture' – to utilize their offensive phrase about Karl Popper, they are both of them 'fluent ideologues'. To begin with Blackburn: where Conquest sees sociology as the selective documentation of a Leftist prejudice, he sees it as the veil drawn across bourgeois social reality. Maybe it is sometimes both and most often neither. By extensive quotation out of context he aims to show how bourgeois sociology is managerial and operational in its tendency, uncritical in its perspectives, bogus and stifling in its rigour, refusing all fundamental structural vantage-points and embracing the common-sensical appearance rather than the dialectical essence. He takes a semi-justified swipe at the vocabulary and assumptions of social equilibrium theory, and claims that revolutionary movements are characterized as structural strain and stigmatized as irrational, particularly by the use of a term like 'charismatic' (yet precisely this question as to how far it is right to employ the terms rational and irrational is debated within sociology for example, Jarvie's *The Revolution in Anthropology*.) All contrary possibilities are ignored by bourgeois sociology as excluded by the limitations of social action *per se* (rather, that is,

---

teachers, whereupon the teachers write model answers. Students compare their answers with the model, and then vote on the results.

[4] For a short compendium of the contradictions in a book whose favourite word is 'contradiction', see Christopher Ricks, 'Student Thought', in *The Listener*, March 13 1969.

than by the specific limitations of the capitalist system). The really significant alternatives are avoided by linking Fascism and Communism in the single odious category of 'totalitarian'. Sociologists try to make up for a boring restricted political style and non-participatory public life by idealizing the family as 'a little democracy', the main evidence cited for this being some articles in the London *Evening Standard*.

Reading Blackburn one might not realize that for every tendency cited there is a contrary tendency, and that his broader criticisms are the small change of every bourgeois seminar. Moreover, it is no more plausible that sociologists should ignore the possibility of revolution in Asia, Africa, and Latin America than that Herbert Marcuse should ignore the possibility of no revolution in 'the West'. And, after all, one of the most functionalist analyses is precisely that provided by Marcuse himself when he pessimistically notes the incorporation of the working class into the capitalist system. If bourgeois society were as pervasively hegemonic, as totally inter-related and as capable of specializing in the 'confiscation' of rebellion as Marcuse and his followers suggest, then the despised functionalism of bourgeois sociology is more nearly vindicated than ever before (at least in the supposedly unfavourable context of advanced industrial society).

The most obvious technique employed by Blackburn is the utilization of a type of slippery evasion involved in 'to some extent', 'perhaps', and 'in many respects'. Add this to selective quotation, guesses as to what Talcott Parsons might have meant based on what Kornhauser did mean, and the occasional straight inaccuracy,[5] and you have a perfect formula for professional defamation and ideological distortion. Take the following piece of misrepresentation:

> Social scientists often proclaim a commitment to 'scientific values' but rarely consider the nature of such values to be a problematic question.

This is just *untrue* since social scientists are obsessively concerned

---

[5] *Viz.*, the claim that schizophrenia coming to the attention of the medical authorities is found in 20 per cent of families; in fact, it is 4 per cent at the most.

with this question; and for Blackburn to select crude versions of positivism as paradigmatic for social science reduces his polemic to an absurd level; it is no wonder he so disdains the notion of objective fact. Or take the claim that bourgeois social science is wedded to the notion that everything is as it appears. Quite apart from the Marxist element which exists *within* social science as a fructifying and dialectical component, has he never read Durkheim or Weber, or their modern variants? What about the notion of 'latent function'? What about the sociology of knowledge? Ever heard of residues and derivations?

To turn to Perry Anderson. Like Robin Blackburn he has just that kind of fast slippery mind in which the facts have as much chance of catching up with the self-validating schema as winded empirical greyhounds have of catching a metaphysical electric hare. Moreover, Anderson positively justifies his selectivity by claiming it is intentional. But when does selectivity become sheer distortion? How wrong do you have to be in order to be just wrong? Take for a start the thesis that there is an 'absent centre' in British culture and that no social scientist of an original calibre was ever thrown up in Britain. This is just patently not the case: leaving the Scots aside, Herbert Spencer is a major figure by any standards, and certainly the equal of Pareto. The achievement of L. T. Hobhouse in comparative developmental sociology is a massive one (even though its author was philosophically within hailing distance of the anaemic British idealism Anderson so much dislikes). Similarly, Morris Ginsberg. Or take the suggestion that sociology is a poor cousin of social work: what kind of ignorant nonsense is this? And so on and on. Britain produced no important Marxist thinker: well, it depends on what you mean by 'Marxist', but one of the central components of Marxist thinking, the theory of imperialism, was contributed by J. A. Hobson (1902), and Christopher Caudwell's *Studies in a Dying Culture* (1938) is a significant intellectual achievement.

In Anderson's view the 'white emigration' of Continental liberals and conservatives dominated the gap left by the 'absent centre', exploiting their superiority to and their affinity with British culture.[6]

The case is best made out for philosophy, though as usual Anderson shuffles the time-scale around to suit his purposes. Wittgenstein has only dominated English philosophy since the war, and the argument ought to be that he suited North Oxford rather than that he suited England. Moreover, the counter-attack on this domination came from Ernest Gellner, who represents the hated liberal utilitarian tradition and who incidentally produced *Thought and Change* (1965) which on the premises of this article has no right to exist. Anderson actually notes that the attacks in several fields come from *within* the culture and from *within* the liberal tradition (Carr, Leach, Gellner) – but then blithely carries on as if there were no need to revise his argument.

If that argument is half true for philosophy and for North Oxford, it is absurd for history. You cannot use L. B. Namier as a 'white emigrant' who conveniently 'stands in' for English history. As Anderson knows perfectly well there is a Marxist school of history in England: Hill, Hobsbawm, Thompson, Dobb, Saville and others. And what about the achievements of English *economic* history, to take just one aspect highly relevant to his thesis? Whatever would his contentions have looked like if he had selected the native Tawney and not the emigrant Namier? (Or *Sir* Herbert Read[7] in aesthetics and William Empson in literary criticism?) He is good on some individual thinkers (Namier and Leavis, especially) but wrong about the discipline and therefore wrong about the significant inter-relation between the disciplines. And of course he does well to omit the sciences and the arts on the spurious ground (at least for the arts) that they are not appropriate to this context. The culture that produces a Henry Moore, a Barbara Hepworth or a Benjamin Britten has a vigorous continuity and is scarcely 'becalmed'.

[6] The accusation that we neglected the tiny 'red emigration', for example, F. Antal and Isaac Deutscher, is a bit thin. Deutscher's Trevelyan Lectureship at Oxford in 1966 was not without honour. Antal was not ignored; and in spite of our becalmed cultural condition, sales of his books have trebled since he died.

[7] We knight the native rebels as well as the migrant conformists.

What might more plausibly have been argued (only it is a platitude and fashionable novelty is preferable) is not that chloroform and amnesia characterize our stagnant island but that its critical tradition does not aspire to the premature syntheses, to pretentious explanations of Everything, and to naturalistic metaphysics; nor does it harbour the totalitarian decisive 'cultural hegemony' of Revolution of which he speaks with such misplaced adulation. And it does lack something of the underlying *angst* which some people find so profound. No doubt we have never been sufficiently split open in our psychology to be taken in by Freudianism. But Anderson constantly wobbles between saying that a becalmed society is either culturally mediocre or afflicted by amnesia. Yet Bertrand Russell was a product of the 'calm': he 'dominated' English philosophy up to World War II, and he was neither mediocre nor given to amnesia. In any case there is a position *between* 'revolutionary hegemony' and 'chloroform'. No doubt Anderson despises it for that reason. Yet the tradition of critical empiricism from Booth to Titmuss is no mean succession, and however much the New Left may sneer, it just so happens that such people have made England a fairly tolerant, decent, and pleasant place to live in. Perhaps that is why the white emigrants came here after enjoying the fruits of 'totalization'. And though Blackburn may complain about illegitimate or blurring conflations, totalization is always first cousin to totalitarianism.

How is it that the new Left has not been brought by historical events to reflect more deeply on why it is that Czechs find them and their German and French *confrères* so absurd? The reason is they know what genuine repression is as distinct from the bogus repressions of tortured fantasies. As a member of the Czech Communist Party put it to me recently, 'I have discussed these things with your new Left and now they don't want to speak with me any more . . .' Very wise of them. Isn't it curious (or to use their phraseology, 'It is no accident . . .') that the Marxist tradition is only interesting in the despised West, whereas wherever it triumphs it establishes a 'cultural hegemony' nearer to death than chloroform?[8] If I may quote from a Marxist colleague in Eastern Europe: 'How lucky you are in the West to be able to discuss freely and critically such important matters as power and prestige, the role of the military, the extent of educational equality – when we are restricted to such managerial matters as the morale of the labour force. You know, we are more totally alienated than any other intelligentsia! We do not dare to think. It is our supreme achievement to survive . . .' The truth is that so-called bourgeois sociology, here and elsewhere, discusses precisely the important problems just mentioned; and it is also true that even the most dissident and self-alienated in the Western democracies are able to do more than survive. Some of them even produce readable books on Student Power and sell 25,000 copies in the first week. It seems our battered old culture is as kind to red natives as to white emigrants. Playboys of the Western world, unite! – You have nothing to lose but your royalties . . .

[8] The New Left turns a blind right eye to the mere historical appearance of Marxist régimes. But dialecticians who can tell essences from appearances can also divine that they are the *true* revolutionary missionaries and it will presumably be with *them* that libertarian revolution will achieve its finest flowering.

12. Order and Rule

*This essay, originally given as an inaugural lecture in October 1972,
attempts to mount a sustained critique of the spontaneity cult so central to
most of the issues raised in the other essays. It is designed to be read at
various levels: at one level it indicates the social a priori of freedom and
creativity, at another it states some preliminaries to an incarnational
theology rooted in particularities of place and time.*

*By the time this inaugural lecture was delivered the explosiveness of
the experiential ideology had receded: there were none of the attempts to
shout down criticism characteristic of three years previous. Overt dis-
ruption had passed to the polytechnics, who were reproducing with some
faithfulness the passé phenomena that once excited the L.S.E. (I had to go
to Bath Technological University to find slogans like 'Do not adjust
yourself: there is a fault in reality'.) But the psychology of experientialism
remained and its assumptions had passed so much into the ordinary
pabulum of advanced thinking that people no longer recognized the
debatable character of their pronouncements. It had become 'natural' and
uncritical.*

In this essay I am going to be inquisitorial about a popular local
heresy. The word 'heresy' means choice and this particular heresy
is the cult of choice. An inquisitor normally busies himself with
consigning the bodies of heretics to the flames but my purpose is
limited to subjecting the body of heretical doctrine to enquiry. In
the traditional manner of inquisitors I shall assume that heresy is
unbalanced truth. The heresy of choice is derived from sources
most of which I approve: the Protestant notions of conscience and
personal decision, the liberal concept of individual freedom, the
existential search for authenticity, the Romantic conception of
genius, the psychoanalytic ideal of autonomy. An even more

fundamental source may be the Christian belief in the soul and the idea that the only fundamental distinction amongst men is between the damned souls and the redeemed.

I should make it clear that I do not regard the heresy of personal choice as the worst error likely to come the way of a conscientious inquisitor. Perversions and exaggerations of necessitarian doctrines are usually even more dangerous. There is, for example, the vicious notion that the ordered universe of social relations is part and parcel of the mechanical necessity of the world of nature. There is the sinister belief that human beings will be dragged into freedom behind the chariot wheels of history.

Let me open the case by briefly indicating the nature of the heresy under enquiry and the kind of argument to be pursued against it. As regards the latter, I shall suggest that the proponents of 'freedom' and choice ignore its preconditions. They reject the social *a priori* of personal identity: an order of rules and roles. They associate freedom with chaos. I shall defend order as the basis of freedom and argue that the rhetoric of freedom needs to be carefully qualified. These qualifications will be stated in relation to the specific nature of particular institutional orders: the family, the school, the church and the university. Every order has its own rule. They can also be stated in relation to the specific 'order' to which man belongs generically: above the beasts and below the angels. Man is neither so context-bound as an animal nor so context free as an angel. The nature of man involves an embedded freedom. I shall also argue that to ignore this embedded character of human potential leads to further dangers: an exaggeration of the possibility of being context free *and* of the degree to which contemporary humans in our society are bound to context. The insistence that men can be as angels, neither marrying nor being given in marriage, leads to the claim that our contemporary social order programmes men like beasts. By the same token it aspires to universal knowledge and experience total relativity.

Let me now expound the basic logic of the heresy of choice. The logic of the spontaneous self seeks its sole context of identity in a pure humanity, and in order to achieve this human essence it rejects all distinctions based on role, whether articulated in a vertical hierarchy or rooted in division of function. The only relevant distinction is ontological, between those who recognize their pure humanity and those who do not. The former are real people, conscious of their alienation; the latter are alienated automata, barely aware that such is their condition. They respectively approximate the redeemed and the damned. Their category is determined by their answer to the question: to be or not to be.

Real people exist in two modes: the one and the all, humanly unique and submerged in the universally human. It follows they cannot be categorized in terms of function, even and specially biological function, or assessed in terms of graded competence. The sacred psyche admits no more or less. Essence like God is not divisible. There is distinction of persons without division of substance. Enumeration based on accidental characteristics is anathema and so is organization based on purposes not one's own. By an odd transposition of classical individualism there are no purposes beyond the wishes of the person. The subject is not to be subjected. He steers himself entirely by an internally generated system of relevance. And by another transposition of classical individualism these systems of relevance lock automatically into each other, as it were 'by an invisible hand'.

All externally imposed purposes are engines of inauthentic being: powerful engines no doubt but in the last resort unreal. Even the external power of greater knowledge and experience must be rejected since all experience is to be personally owned not passed on. There must be no mechanical transfer of knowledge. The noumenal self is born free and is already full of experiential potency. Traditional modes are mere automatic transfers: everyman must start afresh. Knowledge cannot be cumulative. Learning is an expanded awareness which requires no more than the provision of an arena for exploration. An educational system cannot proceed beyond making something available. The subject cannot be subjected; mastery is not conveyed by masters. The relationships of educational production are egocentric. One is not taught by somebody nor does one master a recalcitrant externality: the individual enters into an absorption of environment as a personally appropriated totality.

Totality, whether the totality of humans or the totality of the experienced environment is the logical complement of uniqueness: the all complements the one. This means that there are neither separate subjects to be acquired nor separate senses by which they are apprehended. As in mystical experience each sense merges into one: touch, sight and sound run one into each other. Human beings touch each other to experience the purity of their substance. The All of the world is as God and the unique persons participate in the All as constituent elements of the Godhead. Thus God is not distinguished: the category of God set over against Man vanishes with the distinction between God and Nature. Religious feeling is oceanic. To be submerged in the ocean is to return to the condition of the child before the world was subdivided by social fiat. He enjoys a participatory democracy of elemental awareness. The child-like condition is as innocent of moral guilt as it is of categories, indeed of modulated language. Thus there are no built-in, derived structures of moral sense, only heteronomous mobile centres of personal sensibility. Nothing can be predicted of such a creature because the genuine response is immediate and therefore random. Once this randomness is achieved external moral programming and social organization are rendered impossible. Social life returns to a condition of nature.

Clearly, for those seized by this logic of the spontaneous self the existence of particular institutional orders and of a specific character attaching to each is undesirable. Families and schools are condemned as vehicles of received tradition and of prior, unexperienced cumulations likely to weigh down the buoyancy of the self. Furthermore they are channels of sub-cultural variation and this offends against the primacy of the single human totality. Churches too are condemned because they proclaim freedom yet try to achieve it by the most complex treacheries against the self. They divert the impulse to authenticity into the silted channels of alienated tradition and superimposed forms: received rituals, automatic repetitions, frozen icons of freedom, stories from which the dynamism has been drained. They freeze the person in the name of salvation and this is the most seductive of all treasons against being. They turn personal existence into an externally projected essence composed both of all the images of genuine being *and* all the forms of repressive externality: the free is encapsulated in the superimposed, the transcendent person subjected to a transcendent God, who legitimates all the varied orders of repression by himself constituting a separate order of Being, wholly other. The discipline of divesting oneself of the love of created things in order to be united to this otherness is the exact converse of total and easy immersion in the All. Thus Christian baptism is the first step made by the Other in a sequence which ends in total alienation. The only true baptism is natural birth.

Conventional Science goes the way of religion. After all, it claims to be based on rational cumulation, a sort of coral reef to which each human adds another dead, inauthentic body. It affirms external rules which can only be conquered by acts of profound subjection. It posits an order to which personal vagary is irrelevant. In fact, science represents the apotheosis of mechanism. To take up the role of scientist is to cut out one's human flesh and experience a fall into mere cognition. And along with this subjection to the cognitive goes an exploitative mastery, polluting the innocence of the natural, naively experienced world. The personal poetry of experience is transmuted into a bureaucratic, colourless prose in which language goes abstract. There is no more choice about it than a sequence in logic. For conventional science Nature is abstracted data; for human persons it is a rounded response to the world, given not as data but ex gratia, by grace. Natural laws are like social and moral rules and they are to be broken down by overwhelming personal grace. Scientific revolutions should work not by rational suasion but by personal conversions, by turnings to new paradigms based on the mysterious movement of grace. Social science likewise, should be the exploration of the context of personal life, the explication of the activity of the subject. One cannot rise above the saturated contextuality of personal life to an external view composed of rational comparisons. Situations like humans are incomparable over cultural space and time. Cultural space like cultural time is discontinuous. Total immediacy produces total relativity. Grace is supplemented by faith in the apodictic reality of the experience of oneself and others. The dogmas of natural grace and natural faith (or faith in the natural), supplant the external eye of abstracting rationality. Thus the dogma of personalism hangs over the abyss of scepticism and relativity.

The arts too are condemned by the dogma of spontaneity. There are no pre-existing moulds or cumulated technical means to constitute the necessary conditions of expression. Just as there are no subjects, and no distinct modes of experience so there are no distinctions between the arts, or between critics and performers, or performers and audience. The critical act of dividing up levels and modes and qualities of experience for dissection based on circum-scribed analytical purposes creates illusions of delimited, limiting sectors of reality which feed alienation. Creation annihilates criticism and vice versa. The genuine is the sole criterion. Like the critical act, the creation of acts within plays destroys the free play of the self. The separation of audience and players brings about a false division between the active and the passive mode. A set piece, designed for repeated performance freezes spontaneity because real freedom is literally ex-tempore. Indeed, it is temporarily ex-literal. Everyone is an artist and poet and there can be no function-ally distinct professions of artists and poets. The totality of persons must participate and their participation must be a continuous creation, not a repetition of set roles. People who have been made whole cannot repeat parts. There are no models or monuments, permanent exemplary achievements embodied in 'classics'. Art is not an artefact. Arts, like facts, are abolished.

What finally are the relationships between the personally free and the socially bond? The words with which the free label the condition of the bond are conformity, conventionality, paternal-ism, authoritarianism. These labels are the only permissible ones; all other labels utilized in conventional society are superimposed prophecies which defeat the self. If the self *is* defeated it is because it has been subjected to labelling by those who themselves have been defeated by incarceration in an externally imposed system, by incorporation in families, schools and churches. It follows that those who reject established social forms or have never been ex-posed to them are better candidates for authenticity than those who conform. Deviants are at least potentially genuine people; conformists have relinquished even the possibility of authenticity. Pejorative labels superimposed by conformists are almost guarantees of authenticity: the mad and the criminal are authentic prophets defeated by the inauthentic prophecies. They are the victorious defeated by the defeated. The mad and the criminal have achieved the first pre-requisite of genuine being: rejection of the rules of normal intercourse and of distinctions based on such contingent features as territory and property. Real humans have no properties and recognize no proprieties. Those who make everything their own can own nothing in particular.

Such is the logic of the spontaneous person: it embodies the totality of experience in the immediate present. It is of course, an ideal construct, a piece of social logic to which I've given an intellectual unity it usually lacks in real life. In order to criticize this notion I am going to present another ideal construct based on a quite different notion of freedom. I am going to defend masters and mastery, disciplines and discipleship, habit and continuity, the located and the familiar, the bounded and the particularized, rules, roles and relations. George Herbert's great poem on 'Prayer' – that most immediate and total encounter of the naked self with another – speaks not only of 'church bells beyond the stars heard' and 'the bird of paradise' but calls prayer 'Heaven in ordinary; man well drest'. I want to speak for the ordinary and the common, for man well dressed as well as naked. I am not, of course, against nakedness as such; my contentions concern time and place. The special grace of nakedness is only safeguarded provided it does not aspire to become a universal condition.

Before I move to a consideration of the various institutional orders and to the 'rule' on which they may be based let me pause for a few paragraphs of premeditated play on the words 'order' and 'rule'.

A rule is an instrument of measurement, something which enables you to take the measure of something or somebody. A rule indicates the existence of a regularity, something which enables you to anticipate and therefore to act. A rule is the basis of social regulation, something which tells you where and who you are in relation to a social universe. The activities of grasping, acting, anticipating, and of knowing where and who you are depend on the existence of rule. Men need rulers.

When we say something happens 'as a rule' we refer to statistical and social normality: to that which is usual in nature and accepted in social life. Unless things occur 'as a rule' then nothing is familiar. Familiar things go together as a family and a family is both a classificatory scheme in nature and an intimate conjunction of persons in society. Familiarity breeds: it is the necessary though not the sufficient condition of creativity in our relation to nature and it is the optimum context of creativity in the moulding of persons. Rules, families, classifications are concerned with belonging and by extension with what is proper: properties in nature and pro-prieties in social relations. A property in nature is what belongs to what and property in society is what belongs to whom. It is the basis of grasping the appropriate action in a given context. What belongs to whom further indicates the mode of behaviour which is somebody's due: his due is our duty. And duty is based on the notion of a rule.

The word cognate with rule is order. An order has a rule. Rule and order are each others spiritual familiars. An order is the exercise of the powers of a ruler; it is also a discerned set of complex relations and beyond that it is the basic notion of a universe of such relations. In the social universe an order is a set of likely relations involving both hierarchies of power and esteem and appropriate division of functions. In terms of hierarchy a man performs the duties proper to his order; in terms of function a man who is 'under orders' or 'in orders' is set aside for a particular purpose. To elaborate on the ecclesiastical instance the man 'in orders' is also the *ordinary*: both the exercise of the common and the proper (that is, the usual and the different) depend on the existence of the ordinary.

I mentioned purpose: parallel to the phrase 'as a rule' there is the phrase 'in order to'. We do some things in order to achieve others in the future. Thus the concept of 'in order to' is the basis of giving an historical account of human activity and relates to the essence of history, that is, the *order* in which things occurred. Dates are crucial to history and to any detection and understanding of order in human affairs whether we are concerned with a crime or a civilization.

Let me now turn to the first institutional order for which I want to specify a rule: the family.

The family is the first source of identity, since it identifies those who make it up and its senior members are models for identification. Identity is built up on a process of identification *by* and identification *with*. Creativity begins with moulds and models and gradually achieves originality by variation on the given. There is no guarantee that the moulds and models are good ones, but the alternative is a vacuum or oscillation. A model is a stable sculpture carved out of chaos. It resembles an intellectual model in that it is the first pre-condition of creative variation. From it the child derives the very notion of coherence, of certain things going together and belonging to each other: it is the basis of the notion of 'character'.

The family is a form of going together and belonging, and the model of 'relations' it sets out is superimposed. All models are superimposed on flux. They are rooted in a decision. The necessity of choice so far as parents are concerned demands a firm decision about the nature of the model they provide, concerning what things go together, relate and belong. They designate by their own creativity who belongs and what belongs to whom. They themselves are existential cowards if they do not decide, and moreover their decisions are the necessary though not sufficient pre-condition of equality and justice within the family. There *may* be injustice on account of authority, but there can be no justice without it. Justice in the family is not the consequence of the mutual adaptations of one child to another any more than justice in society has been the consequence of the adaptation of the weak to the strong. In any case the very refusal to provide a consistent model involves the imposition of a model. The refusal to give cues sets a pattern of cuelessness.

There are two ways of providing authority: it can be either superimposed by fiat or built up by habit. To build up a pattern of justice by habit requires *stable* decision making: the outlines of a model once drawn need to be maintained. The model may be filled in, supplemented, extended, modified but the outline must remain firm. Children are drawn into this outline, and define themselves in relation to it. Once the definition is clear and the habits derived from stability achieved they can be invited and co-opted into the process of varying the model. This is genuine paternalism: the process of fatherly induction into the possibility of creative variation. The exercise of personal option depends on co-option. There is of course a limit, because complete co-option can destroy the possibility of creative rebellion. There is a point at which the superimposed nature of the original model must be allowed to become clear, both in order to maintain the integrity of the original parental decision and in order to ensure the integrity of children who desire to make an alternative choice. Their choice must be accorded the dignity which belongs to an Either-Or.

This alternative depends on superimposed decision in another sense: the firm demarcation of what belongs to whom and of private areas which are the sacred thresholds of personal integrity. In this way the family imparts the notion of distinction as well as that of integrity: it defines the common and the individual. By authoritative decision the concept of complex personal structures is made available. Just as the rhythm of the church's year divides common from festive, so the rhythm of the family devises varied space and delineated, shaped periods. It defines limits and opportunities: the play pen is a limit and an opportunity; bed-time is a constriction which guarantees the right to sleep.

The dependency relation of childhood is very inimical to arrangements based on the logic of the spontaneous self. The requirements of survival require pre-emptive decisions and the requirements of economy in decision-making suggest using ready-made cultural modes rather than the confusing invention of new ones. Thus the universal openness of the child is pre-empted willy-nilly by a name, a nation, a role-definition, a place and a set of normal cultural recipes. Where there are siblings equality and justice according to role, aptitude, interest and age depend on the firm exercise of authority. Both the psychological health provided by stability and definition and the needs of justice are rooted in authority and hierarchy. If participatory democracy were instituted in the family it would have the usual consequence: unidimensional determination by peers. That this consequence is indeed usual becomes clearer if we turn to the second order I wish to consider: the education system.

All education should of course, call forth the personal element from teacher and student and has a co-operative aspect. But the ideology of the naked self re-capitulating the process of human learning in his own experience is a wasteful tactic in which the waste is only partly avoided by a covert manipulation replacing the older, overt manipulation. Nor does it succeed in its objective: the person exposed to this method either flounders from lack of direction or is subject to a process of detailed suggestion which leads him to expect and require an environment of persistent support. Whichever occurs, independence of mind and self-determination are not really encouraged. Self-determination emerges more easily when the person is gradually, clearly, overtly, firmly inducted into responsible roles, transferable rules, ordered relations. Learning by osmosis is intended to permit the intuition of general concepts but in fact only succeeds in saturating the person helplessly in a *totally* particular context. A child intuiting a whole sentence is unable to read for himself a single word.

But not only does the child need rules in learning but he requires location in space, fixed points in a room and a day, boundaries marking transitions. Else he ends up the day not only bored with lack of overt difference between times and subjects but sick of the strain of choice. Free expression is easily boredom compounded by strain in which only the children whose home backgrounds teach firm hierarchies of choice and sequences of achievement survive. Boundaries of time, place, role, subject and sequence provide a child with the preconditions of self-definition and self-determination. Not, of course, that boundaries need be rigid but a child should know his 'place'. To say 'go to your place' could be a sharp rebuke under the older system of discipline; but a child should at least *know* his place, because those who do not 'know their place' have no place they can call their own. A demarcated, set, private place is only secured by the firm exercise of *authority*: authority is therefore the basis of a bounded and hence secure location of the self. The alternative to authority is not self-regulation but regulation by peer-group, other-determination, and if authority thinks it can avoid pre-empting the decisions which define a culture's modes and boundaries it only hands the individual over more securely to domination by the norms of local and peer-group culture – a culture which probably does not contain within it the seeds of its own self-criticism.

A school needs to be 'marked' in several senses. A child should be, 'marked', that is seen in his place. His work needs to be marked that is placed and located according to a standard of worth, else he has no mark at which to aim. The school organization needs to be 'marked' in that demarcated areas are created by function and occupant so that chaotic flow is canalized and checked by sacred spots and personal reservations. Enough has to be decided for nine-tenths of life to be gratefully experienced as 'taken for granted': only when whole ranges of things are 'understood' can anything be said; only when enough has already been decided is there an area of personal decision.

Let me now turn to my third order: the Church. Of course, the contemporary Church is afflicted by other models besides the existentialist one. It is, for example, affected by the mode in which science affects society. Each area of contemporary social life is impressed, not so much by the *content* of science, as by the *pace* of scientific discovery. The field of education just mentioned feels the need to produce bogus innovation in order to show that it emulates the scientific paradigm; similarly so the Church. In this way the notion of passing on a good from generation to generation is undermined. But it is also undermined from a quite different direction, which is once again the influence of the concept of the naked person continually confronting people with his existential self. After all, in emulating the paradigm of secular innovation the Church has rather little to offer except administrative reshufflings, flat and often horrible modernizations of language and the occasional gimmicky imitation of media techniques. In religion all the options have been explored already: the latest modernity is in fact the revival of some primitive Shamanism or some ancient and preferably oriental wisdom. The emphasis on the relevant is too clearly complemented by the rapid obsolescence of the merely contemporary. But as regards the naked self the Church can find in that notion a plausible analogue of the naked soul under the eye of God; except of course that the naked self is under the eye of others rather than of the Wholly Other. Thus there appears a curious imitation of the scientific paradigm which is in fact restricted to verbal innovation about the experiencing subject. The forward thrust of so-called relevance coins words to express the aspiration to achieve naked souldom: the vocabulary of meaningful relationship, significant personal encounter. Nothing is signified but one seeks for the personally significant. It is the same bogus innovatory thrust as occurs in education, since there too the vocabulary of 'relationship' represents a new verbal coinage corresponding to remarkably little in terms of actual advance.

But in religion as in education not only do the new words move forward but almost the only content they have is to ensure that education and religion themselves move back. The naked self is in fact a random whirligig deprived of historical content and of the recalcitrant otherness of the world against which the self can be forged. If nothing is passed on, if nothing is given then nothing is received; if no externality in terms of awkward social and physical reality or in terms of cumulating disciplines presents itself then the self becomes an oscillating nullity. One should not conclude that because the dead weight of the past *can* blast present potential, and because the challenge of the environment *can* severely defeat those who try to master it, that the person is fulfilled by following the vagaries proposed by the unhedged psyche. The ideology of the experiencing self is literally *self*-defeating: beyond a certain point the emphasis on *direct* experience diminishes the possibility of experience.

Of course the Church is not so bad as our education system in these respects: whereas the education system attempts to protect the child from experience in the name of experientialism the Church is sometimes capable of realistic forays into the contemporary world and of attempting to work within the sharp

constraints and cramps of actual situations. It is not purely an
arena for indulging the self. Yet the parallels are there and particularly evident where the spheres of Church and education cross.
Educationists afflicted by the ideology of the naked self lose
confidence in their right to socialize, especially if someone
manages to persuade them that civilization is middle class. But the
hesitations of the secular educationist are redoubled in the religious
educationist who finds himself with *nothing* else to impart other
than the ideology of the experiencing self. The modern teacher of
religious education can only move among his pupils proclaiming
that he is as profoundly human as they are; to proclaim himself as
even more human would, of course, be élitist. In any case, who is
to test a claim to extra depth?

The insight of the student, the experiential illumination of the
Gospel depend on rote and rite. What is done by rote and performed in ritual provides the necessary substratum of habit on the
basis of which experience becomes possible. The shortest way to
creativity is habituation to the technical means of expression and
steady soaking in a historical context. In his 'Bluebeard's Castle'
George Steiner remarks on what it must mean for a civilization
to have the Gospels repeated again and again and again in the
central rites of the Church. The model for the Church is not the
logic of the naked self or the systematic obsolescence of scientific
change but – *in part* – a historical model. That model is one of
richness superimposed on richness, of cumulation, of bringing
forth things both new and old, of raising up what has been cast
down, of inserting a new order and a miraculous new birth within the
genealogical table which runs from the first Adam to the second.

Stripping down to the kerygma, stripping off the historic
encrustations of the Church's involvement in culture, stripping
away all that culture might impose on the naked self, is to destroy
both root and flower. In this context radicalism means the destruction of the root. Christ himself becomes no more than the paradigm of a free man. Yet Christ was actually of the root of Jesse. The
Gospel begins with an affirmation of roots: who begat whom. It
affirms universality and freedom by beginning with a genealogical
table based on the peculiar history of Israel. To forget that genealogi-

cal table is to conceive of the Incarnation outside the cumulation of history and away from the particularities of time and place. Christ himself was bounded. The Incarnation depends on that boundary just as grace depends on the law. In the same way the freedom of man depends on our acknowledging that men are not angels. Man's limits are his opportunities, including the arbitrary donations of history and culture. Those who attempt to strip off the successive layers of the onion do not find a true noumenal self at the centre but nothingness: out of nothing nothing comes. Only God creates ex nihilo.

I turn now to the last order I wish to consider: the university. It may seem strange to discuss the university apart from the school and after the Church. But the university differs from the school in that it deals with those who are in early adulthood and (it differs) also since it is concerned with a limited sector of personal development. Moreover, it is, in certain highly specialized areas, affected by the consequences of the knowledge explosion in a way schools are not. So far as its relation to the Church is concerned there is a clear historical connection and a functional similarity. What is catholic and universal in the Church overlaps the breadth characterizing a university. The intellectual clerisy resembles the clergy in its specialized commitment. And so on. However, rather than explore these comparisons I want to consider the implications of the ideology of the spontaneous and masterless self for the process of learning and for the relationships of scholarly production. By so doing, certain other influences derived from individualism will also become apparent, notably the ideology of laissez-faire, the notion of the democratic comparability of all tastes, even the model of political liberalism. All these merge with the cult of spontaneity in their impact on the rule which should characterize the university.

Young people entering a university have usually been members of schools and families while only some of them have acquaintance with churches. In these schools and families they may have been indoctrinated with the ideology of a pure authentic self which, when allowed full expression, enters into self-regulating and harmonious relations with others. Thus they may be the products of a weak version of liberalism whereby laissez-faire is transmuted into personal hedonism and the unbounded unregulated natural commune substitutes for the invisible hand.

But perhaps they are not only creatures of the middle class ideologies corroding school and family, but have also been influenced by two other models, both inimical to the specific purposes of a university. These models are derived from commerce and the media. The first is the market model and it assumes that the satisfaction of personal wants and desires is the only given: the customer is always right. In this model custom does not mean an accepted and understood mode of doing things but a regular demand. Customers habitually make demands. Translated into university terms, students make demands and teachers supply them. After all a salesman must never frustrate a customer. 'Goods' are passed from one person to another rather than a 'good' transmitted from one generation to another. Such goods are not subjected to 'quality control' by the salesman, his business is to minister humbly to assorted likes and dislikes. It is not for him even to enquire whether the assorted items go together or will cumulate into a coherent ensemble over time. Students are now so deeply sold on this principle that they do not even know they have bought it. The consequences of such a principle clearly mingle with the consequences of principled spontaneity, more particularly as regards the relevance of tradition and the way personal relevance may be the basis of any assortment of items.

The second model is that provided by the media. Here the criterion is not knowledge or logical sequence but impact and therapy. This criterion is supplemented by a kaleidoscopic manner of presentation entirely complementary to personal disorder. Excitement is more central than truth, interest and easy assimilation more important than probity of presentation. Many young people take up the cue provided by the emphasis on therapy and come to understand the university as an arena of personal therapy which only differs from the media in allowing activity rather than passivity. They must themselves constitute the drama making news as they go along. Thus if they do not train their intelligences they will at least have released their feelings and put their attitudes on exhibition. In every respect the combined models of the spontaneous self, of supply and demand, therapy and impact, are utilized without regard to context. They generate a common rhetoric which seems immediately convincing. When this is joined to the rhetoric derived from the political sphere, of one man one vote, a convincing reply in terms of the specific nature and character of a university seems impossible.

Yet in fact, a university is less conformable to market and media models than it is to the model provided by structure of the family. Like a family it transmits a good by a prior act of qualitative judgement; like a church it takes a novice, tests his calling and socializes him into a rule of life. As in the family there is a clear hierarchy of knowledge and experience which does not respond to demand but *makes* demands on those who desire to attain the good which is offered. It sets out the minimal conditions which must precede the achievement of certain ends. The custom is not that of the customer but a custom of disciplined criticism.

At this point there arises a problem which has been crucial to all the previous issues. When has personal judgment been developed so that its choices are its own? Libertarianism declares that genuine choice exists from the beginning, authoritarianism states that it never comes into being except for an established élite. Clearly a university cannot take the vagaries of the unhedged psyche as a datum but must make choice at least partly consequent on mastery. Within the particular purposes of a university, choice has some degree of dependence on knowledge. A university must make a preemptive strike in favour of knowledge in order to ensure equality of access to the possibility of genuine choice. Other things may disturb the genuineness of that choice, but choice cannot hope to exist without knowledge. Only when most decisions have been made *for* students can most decisions be made *by* them. Thus authority precedes spontaneity. People who have exercised total freedom of choice from the beginning neither know the range of choice which has been open to them nor realize the range of things they have not become. Total openness leads to absolute closure. Moreover, they can easily suppose that the collection of bits and pieces which seemed initially to be relevant to their spontaneous desires provide an 'education'. Not to know what you are not is as bad as not knowing what you are.

A university thus requires authority and some pre-emptive decision, a demand made by a master that a student achieve mastery, an external standard eliciting the self-determination of those who attempt it, a process of repetitive soaking in the peculiar nature of a subject, and a habituation to its technical instruments. This is the monastic discipline of a discipline: cumulative, demanding, recalcitrant, not always clearly relevant, or pleasurable or therapeutic. The mind explores but the terrain inflicts sanctions on those who ignore maps. The specific grain of a field of knowledge defines optimal paths, constricts the range of alternatives compatible with given destinations.

This is not to say that the terrain is susceptible to only one approach or that the maps provided suggest only one route. It may mean indeed that mastery of a terrain requires sensitivity to the very lack of definition, to the complex overlapping of borders, to the variety of levels at which one may operate, to the varied pay-offs which different types of approach may expect to achieve. In other words, not only is authority in a university a precondition of choice, but mastery is a precondition of freedom which is inherent in the nature of a subject. The personal subject cannot be itself until it masters the subject.

Of course, this is simply to state the minimal logic of the learning and teaching enterprise. The nature of the community itself involves other principles, in that differences in mastery are usually complemented by parallel variations in seniority and by the contrast between a permanent commitment to a vocation and a temporary novitiate. This further tilts the university away from naive egalitarian models based on the procedures of politics, commerce or entertainment or on the logic of spontaneity.

One further element working against the implications of spontaneous choice is the need for benign social processes somewhat apart from the specific requirements of mastery and achievement and able to annul the acerbities of achievement by providing familiar roles. Achievement only bulks large in a destructive manner when stretched over a mechanical grid of educational provision, lacking the support of habitual roles, understood ways of operating traditional procedures, affirmative rituals rooted in the nature of the community.

It is in this context that freedom is most clearly rooted in habit. Without habit there arises a cannonade of continuous prescription and a perpetual testing of boundaries. Territories become defined by persistent raids across frontiers. The individual person cannot settle in such a way as to exercise choice because he needs either to be constantly explaining himself and giving reasons or he has to go into hiding. Personal life exhausts itself in preliminaries. It becomes over-explicit or entirely vacuous, instead of moving freely over paths that are implicit and understood. What is implicit provides the ground for the higher stages of freedom: the right to anonymity as distinct from the inevitability of anomie. Just as identification precedes identity so anonymity completes it. Only a recognized role allows anonymity.

In a university the alternative to hierarchy is not co-operative equality but irresponsible anarchy: 'you in your small corner and I in mine'. Where there is no 'responsible person' on whom rests the weight of pre-emptive decision, there are no responsible persons. The naked self bereft of habituation and of direction tends to become an anarchic monad and moreover a monad complaining he does not know what is expected of him and that he is subjected to multiple pressures from students and colleagues. The naked subject finds that the logic of spontaneity is subjection to the immediacy of others.

In summary, rules, roles and relations are placed by contemporary heresy and potent fashion in opposition to the naked person. This naked person is often conceived as some noumenal self which not only precedes but is distorted by all the particular locations involved in socialization. To recapitulate my understanding of this concept of the naked person I might employ a sexual analogy: it is unclothed, instinctive, spontaneous, uncoerced, immediate. It is deeply averse to the alternative analogy suggested by the process of birth, which is costly, lengthy and imposed. I have argued that this opposition between the true self and rules, roles and relations is misconceived. The true self depends on rules and roles: spontaneity is the last achievement of habit. Of course, differentiated function and hierarchy, or purpose and sequence, or norms and normality may constrict the self severely, but without those constrictions it is extremely difficult for the person to emerge at all. What for radicals is universally given at the beginning and destroyed by the process is actually a costly possible achievement at the end of the process. There are partial exceptions to this, not persons as such but aspects of certain very rare persons, such as a great mathematician or a Mozart. Mozart himself was no angel but so far as music was concerned he was very close to the angelic condition. There *are* traces of glory in our angel-infancy. But most of us are in every respect more than a little lower than the angels. The urge to fly above location in culture, to reject the trammels of the historically given, to be masterless and immediate, is an angelic aspiration which ends in sub-humanity. Thus those who believe in rising above all arbitrary particularities find that they conceive themselves as trapped in a total relativism; those who seek a totally free communication eventually conclude that nothing genuine can be said apart from proclaiming the impossibility of communication.

But to obey the rule of one's order is to discover the possibility of a new order.

Those who have accepted the condition of confinement find they are present at a miraculous birth, limited by time and place, fully human, before which even the angels cover their faces.

13. Parts and Wholes, Objectives and Objectivity

This piece was originally written in Summer 1972 to introduce freshers to what is involved in thinking about society. At the same time it is continuous with the essay on 'Order and Rule' because it turns around a contrast between ritual defined as following out the prescriptions of a pre-ordained order and the vacuum of pure self-expression. A structure of roles is here defended as a necessary constriction which makes possible, though not inevitable, personal freedom, identity and purposeful activity. To act 'as if' and to see and play a part is the precondition of seeing the whole.

You have probably heard the old saying 'God made the country and man made the town'. Actually it is not quite true, but I want to alter that saying and suggest that God made the natural world and man the social world. Since God, we are told, is one, he naturally made a universe: one physical world. Since man is more than one he made a multiverse: several social worlds. Fortunately or unfortunately, man performed this great act of creation without realizing it. He thought somebody else had created the social world, maybe his ancestors, maybe God, he was not quite sure. Moreover, not only was he ignorant of his greatest creative act, he did not realize either that he had created more worlds than one. He thought he lived in a single social universe created by something other than himself, whereas he had himself created lots of worlds.

When he looked at his social universe man saw that it was good. I mean that he thought it fundamentally right and proper. That maybe is why he got misled into thinking that he was only a member of a single universe, because the other universes outside

156

his own were not right and proper. They were different and fell short of what a proper universe ought to be. His own universe was if you like a focus of light, and round about were shades. He divided the light from the darkness, and whereas his own universe was full of light, the others were infiltrated by darkness. This did not mean that his own universe was perfect: it was fundamentally good but not perfect. So he had periodically to try to cleanse it. He had to engage in an act of continuous creation which included purifying his social world of the dross which did not belong to it.

What I've just outlined is a sort of just-so story concerned with the creation of social worlds and maintaining them in good order. What we do in the social sciences is simply this: we see how men create their social worlds, how they forget they did so, and how they try to keep these worlds in good order. Social science studies *creation and order*. By the same token it studies *destruction and disorder*. Creation and order, destruction and disorder are conceived in a variety of ways. Social science studies both how they come about and how they are conceived. For example, the men who live in a particular social universe may see it as basically good, with occasional outbreaks of disharmony. What they have to do is to retune the universe. This means bringing it back to perfection. Men who live in that kind of world find themselves in a cycle, a sort of metaphysical Big Dipper: at the top of the cycle all is part of the original order and then the down-turn starts. Gradually however the inner power of original perfection gathers momentum and the wheel takes an upward turn. It is rather like the cycle of deflation and inflation.

But men who live in *another* social universe can take a more pessimistic view. They can conclude that the social order has somehow or other lost its perfection by a cataclysmic and near-permanent decline. The world is permanently out of tune. Only another cataclysm can restore the great original. They may have various ideas as to how this is to be done. For example, a representative of the great original could come and point the way to recovery. Or the ancestors who made the world could come back and restore it. Or the God who was responsible for the universal harmony which once swayed man and beast, could by a great act recover that harmony. Or, finally, it might be realized that the first creator was indeed man, and that he must make further creative efforts on his own account. This may involve him in acts of destruction before re-creation is possible. True order may require destruction and disorder.

So it comes to this: men create order and disorder, each being part of the other. They conceive the relation of the one to the other in different ways: the idea that the world needs retuning is the way the Chinese usually saw it in the great universe of Chinese civilization. The idea that we have suffered one disaster and must have another before we can recover is the way people have seen it in the great universe of Christian civilization. Now a lot follows from whether you live in a Chinese or a Christian universe. In a Chinese universe the wheel *revolves*, that is it turns round and round. It moves but is static. In a Christian universe one awaits a revolution, a basic conversion. The wheels move forward.

Social scientists are students both of how social worlds are created and what difference it makes to live in one rather than another. They are interested why people come to see the world as one where wheels turn on their own axis, or as one where the wheel moves forward in a fundamental revolution. They are interested in the different consequences which follow in the one rather than in the other. They all believe that men created their worlds and they are interested in why men usually forget it, or why they make no effort to re-create their worlds. They ask: what hides from men their own responsibility for what the world is like now and their ability to change it for the better? They often answer this question by saying that society itself, man's creation, puts a blindfold round the eyes of the creator. They go on to say that this blindfold works by making men suppose that the social worlds are as inevitable as the natural world. Indeed, when men are blindfolded in this way they see their world as 'natural'. Anything else would be unnatural. Men who try other ways of doing things are unnatural. The social world is a *given*, a datum. What is given cannot be taken away. Those social scientists who feel most strongly about this believe that the worst disaster is the one where men forget their own power in creation and recreation. They call the condition of helpless reverence before, 'the given' *alienation*.

Now this is where social scientists begin to disagree amongst themselves. Just now I sketched two ways of seeing the process of order and disorder: the revolving wheel and the revolutionary wheel; movement on its own axis and movement forward. Let me now sketch two views taken by social scientists. I said they were agreed about man creating his social universes and about his ability to recreate them. They are also agreed that men tend to see their worlds as a given. But they are disagreed as to whether or not this taking of things as a given (or if you like taking them for granted), is a good thing or a bad. Those who regard it as bad are those who label it 'alienation'. But others, including myself, are not so sure. Of course, it's not a good thing if you see the social world as unalterable in *any* respect. If you think that your social universe is 'a given' in that sense you cannot act at all. You can only repeat your lines.

Let me take up that analogy of acting and lines, because all the social world is in a sense, a play. I can put the disagreement between social scientists into the mould provided by that comparison. Do we have to accept our parts as 'given'? Now, I mentioned above that we're all agreed that just to accept what is given as if you had no initiative at all is not only wrong but also a mistake. You just *cannot* accept the part or role handed out to you by society and repeat the lines associated with it. You can't be a zombie even if you try. Things are not 'given' in that sense. The nearest you can get to mere repetition is in some kinds of ritual. The actions are prescribed and no words may be spoken but those set down. Both the actions and the words are to be reproduced in a certain way. You use a certain voice, you reproduce a set of actions. This is ritual reproduction and it is not recreation. However, as I've said, you can't spend all your life in a ritual. Societies which use a lot of ritual recognize this by including some 'free parts' in the rite. People are encouraged to act extempore, prescribed order is balanced by creative chaos. So not only is it impossible for you to 'work' without some personal element in what you do, but it is impossible for society to work without what is taken for granted being balanced by periods of free play. So the great play of society depends for its success on a certain amount of free play in the acting, some element of 'play' and flexibility in the mechanism of the plot. There we are all agreed, and perhaps those sociologists who stress the way in which we play a part also stress that a certain amount of 'play' in the system makes the whole production work better. This annoys those who are fed up with the whole production or who want to get rid of plays all together. They regard this element of play in the play as allowing men just enough freedom to seal their doom as independent actors. They dislike above all those systems which allow enough disorder to ensure the maintenance of order. It's just like a school which allows the pupils to work off steam in playtime so as to ensure they won't object when they're brought back and made to sit behind neat rows of desks.

So far I have argued this: to be part of a repetitive ritual in which you have no initiative at all is impossible as well as undesirable. But to be part of a social production which ensures its own maintenance by allowing you enough freedom not to realize you are bound by your role and by the plot is all too possible. And, some would add, not only possible but *very* undesirable.

But if some social scientists think the play within the play is just a mousetrap what do they want? Do they want nothing to be given, nothing to be taken for granted? Do they want us all to produce ourselves with no guidance from the book whatever? No book and no social production really would mean chaos, and might even destroy the very possibility of anyone being able to express oneself, because after all self-expression is based on a sort of preliminary agreement between two people that what they are going to have is a dialogue.

So let's look at the other extreme from ritual. In ritual everything is *data*, given. Now let us imagine the opposite, where nothing is given. In this situation there is no social production, no roles, no script, no plot, no audience. Everybody does their own thing. They don't merely switch roles from time to time but have rejected the very idea of a role in favour of being themselves.

They don't want to be actors, working through the prescribed scene act by act; they want to be in on the act *themselves*. They want to make their own scene. They are themselves pure beings, totally free persons engaging in a pure act. They don't do what they're told or turn out a good performance: they *are*. They are what they are. Indeed, they approximate to the traditional definition of God as actus purus, the great I AM. These social beings live in their own universe, created and recreated solely by themselves. They are self-made men, great I AMs. Their universes do not intersect other universes, but collide. Self-made men are universes in collision.

Unfortunately, a person who is self-made is no person at all. He is not even a zombie: he is just a vacuum. A self-made man is really a hole in the heart. Pure self-expression finds itself with no self to express. When nothing can be taken for granted then you have no base from which to work: the fabric of creation becomes base-less. What is base-less is impossible: a dream. The idea of pure self-expression is as impossible as the idea of pure ritual; total invention is as unattainable as total repetition. Indeed they're both a kind of dream. A man who is engaged in going through the motions of a ritual seems to be in a kind of dream, because he acts without knowing he is acting. He sleep-walks. Similarly a man who is engaged in pure self-expression is real dreamy: his world is a kaleidoscope of jumbled images, a realm which lacks unity of space and time.

Real plays depend on a unity of space and time or, at least some deference to a specified context of action and a sequence of motives and actions. The text of the play requires contexts and pretexts. The vacuum of pure expression needs to be filled by an ordered universe of social times and social spaces. Social space is the way in which roles intersect: in short social space is *relationships*.

I want to suggest the following, just in case you are getting a bit lost by the analogy of the play: You need a role before you can be a person. You can't act without a part. Being a person is playing a part. It's more than playing a part, but it's rooted in being able to take certain things for granted. You can't acquire an identity until you can identify *with* somebody and be identified *by* somebody. To have identity, to identify with, to be identified, all imply the existence of a role. Roles are good for you and for everyone else.

Let me illustrate. A little while ago on the B.B.C. programme called 'Meeting Point' there was a discussion of the role of roles. Do they constrict us, or do they offer us an opportunity to act, and a base from which we learn to be ourselves? The participants were a housewife who was also a journalist, a university don who had become a friar, and a journalist who had given up working for a newspaper to write for his own pleasure. Alongside these three were people with varied social roles, including a policeman and a nurse. Here then were the people who make up the social play discussing what it's like to have a part. I only want to relate two elements in the exchanges which followed. The first concerned the academic turned friar. He had found that as an academic who was also an ordinary clergyman he had had to live up to people's expectations of him. He had lived in other people's eyes. The result was a life of performing in accordance with the anticipations of others. He had been monitored by the great eye of society, but had not met other people eye to eye, I to I, in personal dialogue. His part in social life had evoked only a part of him. Becoming a friar had set him free to be himself. What he did as an ordinary clergyman and a don had been fairly closely prescribed by a structure of expectations. So, when he met a student it was for a specific purpose, to discuss an essay, consider a point of logic, assess the sequence of an argument, comment on the reliability of the evidence. Similarly when he met a parishioner he acted within limits set by their idea of a clergyman: he didn't swear when he stubbed his foot, didn't look like a tramp when walking down the High Street, and so on. And because he was part of a community where he was well known he didn't have any of the freedom that attaches to anonymity. So he was subject to what social scientists call social control: the fact that he was identifiable in a particular role and that he was part of a community which was not large enough to allow anonymity meant that he was controlled. This wasn't *self*-control: he didn't do these things and wear these clothes because he wished to or thought them morally valuable but by the power of an external social pressure. As a clergyman his presence acted as a constraint on other people: they in turn constrained him (these are, if you like rules about the nature of rules: they act by mutual constraint, and such constraints act most efficiently on the basis of the frequent interaction found in a small community). Becoming a friar had been, in one sense, becoming kind of religious tramp, and this had extended his freedom to be himself, and if he still acted rather similarly to the way he had acted before, this was by interior choice and not because of social pressure. His friar's habit allowed him to *choose* his habits.

So there was an illustration of the constricting power of roles; the other illustration showed how they can liberate a person in order to perform an appropriate action. The nurse said that when she went on duty for the first time in the hospital she had been protected by her uniform (look at those words 'duty' and 'uniform' because they indicate what is 'due' in relation to a role, and the set, socially prescribed means by which the role is identified). As she entered the ward she had felt not a mere newcomer stumbling onto a new stage, but 'just a nurse'. Now at this point Victoria Brittain interrupted critically: 'But surely it's not enough to be *just* a nurse'. The nurse looked a bit uneasy at this criticism, but explained that she had a job to do for which she required confidence in herself and confidence from the patients. Moreover, she required identification. Trust and identification were conferred by the uniform. And given that initial confidence, she was able to play her part and eventually to give a service in which she was involved as a person. Of course that involvement was limited by the nature of the role and that limitation was all to the good: she was not to be involved to the point of fainting at the sight of blood or having erotic exchanges with the male patients. The restrictions of her role made possible the art of healing. It was through that art that she fulfilled herself.

So far I have talked about roles in general; now I want to extend my comments on the social play into two more specialized areas: the political game, the domestic drama. I'm going to look at roles within the family and the roles of politicians. In both areas a role is a constriction partly because of other people's expectations,

TRACTS AGAINST THE TIMES

partly because it must be shaped by whatever goal you want to achieve.

First of all, then consider the family and how people play parts in the domestic drama. This particular drama begins with the welding together of two universes. Two people try to see how they can inhabit one universe. Their roles are not much affected by any particular purpose. They are not out to *achieve* anything or *make* anything except to make something of their lives together. In the technical language of social science we say that their aims are expressive not instrumental. Now here we have what appears to be the maximum room for the free play of persons. They can live together in mutual fantasy, they really can share a world of dreams. But in fact this world of dreams is already structured for them. For one thing the very idea of a world of dreams inhabited by two persons attributing ideal qualities to each other is presented to them by the culture in which they live. At any rate the notion that their dream worlds should be the basis of a common life together for a prolonged period in which children become a responsibility of them both is a general cultural expectation. It is what we call a cultural pattern. A cultural pattern is a sort of mould; it is a template around which peoples' anticipations are cut. This pattern is much more than a generalized expectation. It provides a model for behaviour, a sequence of moves which are sometimes as strictly governed as the moves in chess. And these models and expected moves are not necessarily a misfortune. If two people have an idea of the basic moves that need to be made they can communicate with each other. A game in which there are no rules makes sharing impossible. If I do not know that such and such a move signifies this or that and if I do not know that move 1 is normally followed by move 2, then I don't know how to respond. This is true whether I want to respond positively or negatively. If I want to respond positively I can hand the other player a card saying 'Move on to the next stage'. If I want to protect myself I can direct him to an area marked 'wait'. Moreover, the existence of rules not only controls us both but can protect each participant. I can hide behind a convention, or I can prevent him being hurt by delicately fitting my rejection inside some convention. I don't need to administer a raw hurt.

Of course as the love game goes on the two people involved can use the rules more and more creatively. It becomes a rule that they are allowed to dispense with some of the rules. But as they do so the protecting function of rules and conventions is reduced: each person becomes more vulnerable. Freedom exacts a price in vulnerability. But as the rules of the preliminary engagement between persons are put aside (according to a set of rules allowing them to be set aside), so freedom is constrained within another theatre. This is a world of models of the other person, a stage which is full of revolving and receding mirrors. So we are not yet in a world of pure persons but in a world where people are seeing each other as reflections of themselves, and of other people, particularly those people who provided them with their first models for the roles of husband and wife. Indeed, a man loving a woman sets her against several models superimposed one on another: the cultural ideal, the actual cultural expectation (less than the ideal), the way his mother played her part in relation to *her* husband, and the way she played her part to *him*. And then there are the standards of wifely beauty, bearing and behaviour expected by those who are his friends and peers: the sub-cultural expectations. One might say that he loved whatever shaped up to these expectations as much as choosing the loved one and measuring her against what he expected. So not even love is totally free; not even sexuality is naked.

Now let us turn to what looks like a very different subject: politicians and Northern Ireland. This is a case of the politics of hate not the politics of love. It is public not private, large-scale not small-scale. It is our domestic tragedy not our domestic comedy. Yet there are common elements between the family and politics. In Ulster we watch the performance of a drama as close to ritual as a Greek tragedy. Greek tragedies are plays in which all the spectators know the plot and in which events move relentlessly towards a foreordained end. Such a ritual as we watch in Ulster not only keeps repeating itself in the present but is a presentation to the present of a remote past, historically and psychologically primordial. In that past there is some primal act of injustice, a first murder, a filching of something believed to be a birthright. These paradigmatic events have generated complementary murders and injustices, which spiral through centuries, soaking every subsequent event in the colour of blood. History both consists of periods, cumulative and different, and of repetitive cycles. The cycles are cycles of hate. Indeed, many marriages are like that: daily recitations of an office of violence against the other person which occur within cycles from which there is no escape. Ulster is a daily office of violence whereby the past is recited. The office is not only recited but sung in songs which celebrate and reprobate. Ritual processions pass and repass each other, like crocodiles of encapsulated hate. Each procession is part of the march of the remote past into the present, so much lava welling up from unforgotten centuries to move remorselessly into the contemporary world. So history is contemporary. This history is not the recorded chronicle of events, or traceable periods with this or that defining character, or explanations of the sources of social change, but a reference back to key symbols of differences in power and identity. Just as in marriage it is not the actual events which matter, or even the different demarcated stages, but the impact of a litany of hate, the raising up of the sacred symbols of rejection. Thus tiny events can trigger – literally – the heaviest burden of meaning. A fragment of cloth, orange or green, is an identity, a religion, and a history. A man labelled orange or green becomes a mere historical cut-out: a stereotype. His humanity is prejudiced, prejudged by a label. Moreover, he lives up to that prejudice and confirms it. His trigger triggers his enemy who responds to the confirmation of a prejudice by acting so as to deepen it. As in marriage so in Ulster every act in the tragic play shows the antagonist to be just what the protagonist had always thought him to be. They never change. Each stands posturing in the receding mirrors of all their yesterdays, deriving their judgments from their pre-judgments. Judgment is executed: *people* are executed in accordance with that judgment. The terrible thing about such judgments is that they are often just because the prejudices have made themselves true. The trouble with prejudices is that so often they have become nearly true. Prejudice is error in the process of becoming truth.

Each side suffers reversals, but is there any suffering which might reverse the process? The active suffering of revolution might reverse the process and move the whole play into a different period, another stage. Or there is passive suffering: the primal murder can be complemented by a man offering to be murdered. Either way men seek atonement. But to be at one with whom? Who are the *true* revolutionaries, with whom a man is to be at one and by whom all can be made one? The Irish Republic, the Provisionals, the official I.R.A., the Social Democrats? What are the borders of unity and of excommunication? Atonement immediately creates a border. The trouble after all is precisely about a border. Every act of union, in politics or in love, creates a terrifying boundary. Even reversing the primal act by passive suffering creates different versions of the atonement: whose is the right understanding of the atonement? After all the trouble is between Catholic and Protestant. Reversals always encounter reversals. New stages repeat cycles; the wheel moves forward and turns on its axis.

Of course, the model of Greek tragedy is only one way of looking at events. Science can use lots of other ways. It can begin with the mere chronicle of events, though even at this level it will find a Celtic Chronicle and an Anglo-Saxon Chronicle as any television news will illustrate. But you *can* reduce drama to the level of deliberate, unemphatic, documented reportage. Or, alternatively you can abstract the dramatis personae and create a model based on calculations of the best move. The theatre in the round is thereby reduced to one-dimensional boards in which Catholic bishops, English Queens, military knights and pawns are so many different potential moves. This places the whole process at one remove, clarifies some elements by removing others, makes irrationality rational. Protestant and Catholic, orange and green become P and C, black and white. By taking the colour out you create a game 'as if' the contestants were cool manipulators of forces, rational calculators of gains and losses. The moves are determined by rationality just as in Greek drama they are predestined by ritual. Either model drains reality of choice. I want to look therefore at models once again in order – eventually – to say something about choice.

I have been writing about plays and roles, rules, models and games. I want to take the terms rule and model and show how they can be used in two senses. These two senses are absolutely central to the social sciences because one sense marks off what is peculiar to the social sciences and the other marks off the area that they share with the natural sciences. Let me begin by using 'rule' in the sense that is peculiar to the social sciences. Man has been described as a 'rule-following animal'. When he plays the game of love and joins in the domestic comedy he is behaving as a rule-following animal. These rules can be summed up in a very ancient saying: 'There is a time for everything'. The rules specify the time and place of whatever we do. They also specify the rules governing the breaking of the rules and the rules concerning what price rule-breakers have to pay. At least, as a rule. The biggest price to be paid is by whoever is determined to break *all* the rules: he is condemned to a long term of incomprehensibility. Some of these rules are embodied in public statements called laws to which the costs of rule-breaking are officially attached. Others, much more numerous, are embedded in culture, that is in the patterns of our living.

But there are other sorts of rules which are rather different. Let me remind you of the rule I mentioned earlier, about the larger the community the greater the possibility of anonymity. This rule can be stated as a formal proposition: the extent of anonymity varies directly with the size of the community. That statement can stand up to inspection and verification provided its terms are defined and appropriate qualifications added specifying under what conditions it might *not* apply. It can even be given a mathematical formulation. Now this 'rule' can of course be 'noticed' in a vague way by all kinds of people, but it is something *outside* the rules they use for personal living. They may observe it in that they notice it, but they do not observe it in that they obey it in their life pattern. It is an external fact *about* peoples' interaction one with another, and they observe it in the way they watch an apple fall rather than the way they observe the law or the Sabbath day. They *experience* it just as they could experience the apple falling on their head but it is *not* a rule of life. They can get out of the way of it by moving

to a small community, but the rule itself is not part of their everyday being, even though it may have everyday consequences for
their life.

Now, let us look at a model. I used 'model' as meaning a kind
of portrait in the mind against which flesh and blood were
measured. That portrait was a flesh and blood portrait, the actual
lineaments of a loved one or a hated one. The portrait had been
internalized, painted on the walls of somebody's heart. But I also
used another kind of model which was an abstraction invented for
intellectual convenience. That was the model I suggested between
the wheel that turns on its axis and the wheel that moves forward.
I compared two kinds of revolution. Now of course those models
in their concrete form live in people's minds. They are a sketch of a
Confucian (or Chinese) view of the world compared with a Christian one, and the full, detailed picture is (or has been), a living
reality to millions of people. But the intellectual sketch is a comparison based on an act of selective observation, and it is a remote
sketch of the living reality to serve a particular purpose, that is
to bring out certain salient core features of which those who know
only one of the systems from the inside are almost certainly
unconscious.

To get to know any reality you have first to be immersed in it
as an experience. You play your part in it, but you do not see the
whole because you are so deeply involved. You are sunk below the
eyes of reason. To get to know that whole you have to learn to
see a map, or if you like make a map of the sea in which you have
been submerged. This map is what we call a model, and once again
it is just a part of the whole. It can be constructed on every kind of
principle, on this projection on that projection. But it remains just
a part. When we construct models and maps of the social world
we are playing a complicated game of 'as if'. It is a pretence, the
object of which is to know the real better. We have to pretend
in order to know the real, select a part in order to know the whole.
Once you have pretended enough to have some idea of the whole
you can dive back into reality and play your part. Indeed you can
be doing both all the time: seeing a part and playing a part, the
two forms of observation constantly playing one into the other.

The laws of supply and demand for example are a very abstract kind of model, a projection taken from an extreme angle, but making them part of your mental space still enables you to be better equipped for the real world. If you are not better equipped by looking at all the possible projections from as many types of angle as possible that is your own fault: you took the part for the whole.

Your life here is one: it is a single universe. But it is played, like the universe of music, in several modes. You have to move between one mode and another, playing a part *in* the whole, seeing a part *of* the whole. You move between your personal project, your own real-life portrayal of yourself, and the complex projections by which we intellectually map the same areas over which we pursue our personal journeys, even our pilgrimages. In both we begin 'as if', taking up a role, taking up a specialized viewpoint overlooking the world. Your life will become more whole if you have learnt how to play a part and to see a part. All creation begins with an 'As if', including the creation of yourself. Father Williams played his part by observing the rules of *his* order, and doing so became a freer man. We, in a different mode, play a part by observation of the rules of the social order, including the rules by which the rules may be changed. By knowing the rules about the rules we too may become freer men.

14.   Can the Church Survive?

This final essay is a re-worked variant of lectures given under the auspices of the Dr. Williams Trust at Swansea and the York University Heslington series. In its first form it was concerned with the question 'Can we have a completely secular society?' and it related the phenomena of student religio-politics to the argument about secularization. It was also concerned with the pre-conditions of the survival of different varieties of religious experience from a highly generalized mysticism to the specific and particularized tradition of the Christian religion. What possible future might Christianity have given that certain fashionable trends of religiosity are so opposed to coherent beliefs, defined institutional boundaries and historically created faith? The essay also criticizes the notion that the fragmented, personal form of experience most common amongst contemporary students is characteristic of our period as a whole. The Marxist 'churches' have restored dogmatic boundaries, institutionalized schisms and localized homogeneity without the profound division between temporal and spiritual which qualified Christian tendencies towards socio-religious homogeneity.

In this essay I want to speculate on the future of the kinds of consciousness natural to homo religiosus in a world which some of my
colleagues in the sociology of religion insist is becoming more and
more relentlessly secular.

I would like to begin by taking as my starting point the situation
in my other main interest, the sociology of music. Indeed, as will
be clear below, I believe the sociology of religion and of music to
be intimately related. Like the sociology of religion, the sociology
of music can suggest the sorts of function served by music, such as
orgiastic stimulation, group solidarity, martial sentiment, and it
can discuss the nature of audiences, the growth of the musical

profession, the characteristic and historical location of particular art forms, such for example as opera. It can concern itself with variations in taste, such as the current revival of the Baroque, the recovery of interest in Bach in the mid-nineteenth century, or the eclipse of Meyerbeer, all of which might be analogous to an attempt to trace variations in the resonance of theological attitudes and ideas. But sociological analysis only skirts the fringe of the musical experience itself. True, it can broadly locate a particular kind of musical experience, and can suggest various sorts of psychological and sociological utility, but the experience remains elusive.

I do not merely mean that sociology cannot adjudicate the validity or worth of such experience, but also that the ability to indicate a social and cultural context only links with the specific quality of that experience in a very loose way, particularly where it is entirely unconnected with words, and exists purely for its own sake, as in a Beethoven Quartet. Indeed, in some music one is above all aware that beyond its presence in a particular historic and social location is a timelessness, a transcending of periods and cultures. This sense clearly links it to important modes of religious awareness. Thus both in music and in religion one points to a particular quality of experience which transcends its context, and by so doing suggests qualities of permanence and eternity. If you are never assailed by this type of sensibility then you are, as Weber declared himself – in a most suggestive phrase – 'religiously unmusical'.

Now if this is so, if there are experiences which carry with them a kind of commanding verity, then to those who are their subjects, the question of a completely secular society is a very odd one. A completely secular society would presumably be one where this type of awareness was absent, and there are no signs that secularity defined in such a way is more dominant now than in the past, or is likely increasingly to dominate the future. Some commentators do believe this is so. Ronald Laing, for example, believes we are more and more estranged from the possibility of such experience, but he can cite no evidence, and he is himself a tiny item of evidence that it is not so. I can well believe that in some societies and in certain situations, or in cultures completely bereft of a continuing tradition bearing explicit witness to the possibility of such experiences, then the availability of these 'commanding verities' is restricted.

But, of course, it is not enough to talk about nameless ecstasies, or that something before which we say 'o altitudo', because though the experience itself may be timeless, the interpretation which men place on it is not. In the past it was often connected with the institution of the Church, and with its coherent frame of affirmation about the nature of life, death and reality, even though there were frequent tensions between the mystic and the Church. Yet this link with religious belief and institutions is clearly not an inevitable one. Marghanita Laski would remind us that atheists too are afflicted by ecstasy; R. C. Zaéhner would sharply differentiate between its profane form, (say) in Richard Jeffreys and its sacred form, (say) in St. John of the Cross. At the same time the explicit link with a religious consciousness is remarkably persistent, and is frequently made at the present time. Let me give only one example, and one which includes a reference to music. In one of the essays in 'Language and Silence' George Steiner writes:

> But it is decisively the fact that language does have its frontiers, that it borders on three other modes of statement – light, music, and silence – that gives proof of a transcendent presence in the fabric of the world. It is just because we can go no further, because speech so precisely fails us, that we experience the certitude of a divine meaning surpassing and enfolding ours. What lies beyond man's word is eloquent of God . . . Where the word of the poet ceases, a great light begins.

Those who have attempted to monopolize the awareness of the people of Soviet Russia have at times acted as if they were afraid that this persistent linkage would be made. There have been occasions, for example, when the chorale preludes of Bach have been played in Leningrad *without* the original titles. It is as if the authorities feared there was a natural point of attachment for such a range of awareness to which it would be wiser not to draw attention. Indeed, this example makes one wonder again about the possibility of some putative secular society of the future, because whoever listens to the music of Bach will be seized by an exaltation looking for a point of attachment, and may then suspect that a title such as 'In Dir ist Freude' gives him the hint about where to look.

But I would go further than this. Not merely does religious ecstasy survive, but to the extent that it does not find a fully transcendent point of attachment, can engage in every variety of dangerous liaison. One may or may not sympathize with certain aims of the student movement, but the power of indiscriminate ecstasy to blow through politics, and give uncontrovertible verity to whatever is the current nostrum or panacea, is only too clear. Take the following quotation from a student essay on the L.S.E. occupation:

> ... Coming as I did from an afternoon of peace and solitude, I began to notice a distinct change in atmosphere as I strolled down Kingsway. Coming up Kingsway, in little groups, were people, young people who were speaking in French and disporting assorted garbs. A cosmopolitan feeling immediately attached itself in my mind to the occupation. And when I got to the School my mind was flooded. Joy and ecstasy overwhelmed me. I was filled with emotions of love and suddenly-realized freedom. I was thrilled by the hotch-potch of people. People. People. All over; all sorts; by the doorway two porters sat in armchairs and listened to the music from a transistor. In the foyer groups of people came and went, passed and re-passed, to and fro. One guy with an orange satin shirt underneath a fur waistcoat and orange satin trousers. Foreign people; long-haired and bizarre-clad people; students and non-students, old men and young, down-and-outs and up-and-comings, home and abroad. We had taken hold of L.S.E., thrown open the doors and said 'Come!' No specifications, just 'Come!' And they came. From Leicester, from Aberdeen, from Newcastle, from Charing Cross Embankment and from Paris ...

Clearly such an experience is not easily combined with a search for workable compromises, or with the disciplines and ordered sequence of rational argument. Ecstasy in this instance acts not simply in its own right, pointing to a transcendent quality or realm, but validates and underwrites a political position and a political action. It is the Divine Right of Kings become the divine right of students. One of the marks of a secular society is supposed to be the non-transcendental reference of its political life. If that is so, then a *fully* secular society is not yet with us. It may even be that each step towards pragmatism in politics elicits a political style based on certain paradigmatic symbols of conversion, perfection and brotherhood. The reminiscence of the second chapter of the Acts of the Apostles in the student's essay is inescapable.

On one occasion, while driving through Haslemere, I picked up a student, and asked him what he was reading. It was Traherne's 'Four Centuries of Meditation'. The temptations put in front of students of English literature are, of course, particularly strong, and I suppose they will go on disturbing the surface of secular society for as long as our literature is read. For, surely it is the case that you do not develop a feeling for Traherne solely on the basis of how he writes as distinct from what he communicates. It is even more unlikely than that you should listen to Bach and be charmed solely by an aesthetic pleasure. But we ought to consider what it is that Traherne communicates, and relate it to another supposed mark of secular society, the disenchantment of nature. Now I willingly concede that my student was well aware of the disenchantment of nature in that he knew that there were no demons in Haslemere woods, any more than there were fairies at the bottom of his garden. I also concede that I do not know how many people there are who read Traherne, though no doubt the number is greater than at any time since the seventeenth century, for a variety of reasons.

But he was reading a type of mystical literature whose vision of the world excluded the ravages of sin, evil and time.

'Certainly Adam in Paradise had not more sweet and curious apprehensions of the world than I. All appeared new, and strange at first, inexpressibly rare and delightful and beautiful. All things were spotless and pure and glorious. The corn was orient and immortal wheat, which never should be reap'd nor was ever sown. I thought it had stood from everlasting to everlasting. The green trees, when I saw them first, transported and ravished me, their sweetness and unusual beauty made my heart to leap, and almost mad with ecstasy, they were such strange and wonderful things. O what venerable creatures did the aged seem! Immortal Cherubims!'

[T. Traherne. *Third Century of Meditations*: 1, 2 and 3.)

If that were merely the existential preference of one student it would not be relevant to the question whether or not a secular society is possible. But it links with a very widespread movement amongst students to see man, nature and society in visionary terms. The reaction against positivism, like Blake's reaction against eighteenth century art, is an insistence on the primacy and importance of vision as set over against quantification and disenchantment.

There are a couple of further points I want to make at this juncture. The first relates to the question as to how 'natural' such an experience as that enshrined in Traherne is. If it were natural in a simple sense then a secular society would be an impossibility: people would just go on seeing 'orient and immortal wheat' whatever happened. Against that it is also true that such a vision of the world is specifically located in mid-seventeenth century culture, and I cannot think of a single example in the early eighteenth century. And now in the twentieth century it makes a particular appeal again. If the particular vision is in some way natural to man, it nevertheless shifts in and out of focus according to a mysterious alchemy of cultural time and place. I am even uncertain as to whether place is not rather important for the availability of such experience. I was myself assailed by just such an experience when I was nineteen years old in Ludlow. I do not recollect its happening in Birmingham. Indeed, I wonder whether the border country of Wales – the Malvern Hills, the Wye Valley and Tintern, Brecon Beacons, Wenlock Edge – does not possess a peculiar concentration of this particular numen.

If we indicate a particular cultural moment and even perhaps a certain sort of environment – a geography of mysticism – which is at any rate *not* Birmingham, then the natural availability of this experience is placed at a remove. On the one hand there is the availability of the Welsh border, the availability of Traherne, but also the more pressing and frequent reality of Birmingham and bus timetables. I am not denying transcendent possibilities even in Birmingham, but I do feel that such an urban environment acts as an inhibition. Should such environments become more and more the norm, then a starkly secular view of the world seems to be increasingly possible.

I would like here to introduce another related point which harks back to the availability of certain kinds of transcendent awareness. I mean that even with the growth of more and more Birminghams there is an immense architectural deposit all over the area once known as Christendom which itself forms an insidious invitation to modes of awareness far beyond the mere aesthetic quality of the buildings. If our society of the future is to be relentlessly secular it will have to cope with this alien architectural presence: with hints of mystery and light merged with the numina of tradition and continuity. What is involved here is the notion of a shrine: something which is held up in perpetuity by being set in a particular appropriate architectural frame. Maybe some secular society of the future, preserving them as monuments rather as we preserve the caves of Lascaux, may sense its mundane priorities silently rebuked by the ancient presence, and enquire what kind of storage such buildings represent. The physical persistence of God's warehouses may provoke a sensitivity to the odd merchandise they contain. What I have been saying so far amounts to something like this. Firstly there may be a natural propensity to sense the transcendent: of that we cannot be certain. Secondly, we know historically that such a propensity varies in its incidence and form with culture, period and place. Thirdly, given that we live in a culture where such possibilities are carried forward 'on the books' (as it were) there is in the deposit of western civilization, its music, literature and buildings, a perpetual invitation to alternative modes of being, which even the grossest ignorance of the precise content of its religious frame, cannot completely obscure.

Nevertheless, content is important, and at the conclusion of my comments I shall argue that not only is content important but questions of truth or falsity. Religion is more than an intimation, and in the traditions of our own culture it has a fairly specific content, conjoined to specific affirmations, which are either true or numbered among the saddest delusions ever to seize upon the human mind. Let me concern myself largely with specific content. Religion, especially, our own traditional religion, rooted as it is in events of history, requires knowledge as well as feeling. Indeed it is not possible to make much sense of it (leaving aside the most generalized feelings of awe and guilt) without a minimum body of knowledge. Such knowledge concerns above all the sacred story, but also the significance of rite, ceremony, enactment and symbol. This is so specific as to depend partly on a decision to educate. Of course it is difficult to eliminate some minimal acquaintance with the core events celebrated, say, at Christmas, and it would be a long time before this knowledge vanished from general culture. Indeed, just as architecture would be a reminder of a certain mode of being, so all kinds of references in general culture would keep a minimum knowledge in existence. This is much less true of the fundamental rites and symbols of the Church. Its ceremonies of innocence and brotherhood, holy baptism and communion, and its symbols of forgiveness and sacrifice, are not immediately 'open' to uninformed inspection. The crises and axes of human life to which they refer, are, of course, always with us, but the precise, historically rooted symbolic formulations of those crises can drift more and more to the margins of modern life until they are out of reach in a tiny ecclesiastical backwater. No doubt access to considerable ranges of western culture may recede with it, and those who wish to retain access to the past will try and preserve a minimum knowledge, but their success is not assured. As classical civilization and its intricate web of meanings has partly disappeared from view, so too may Christian civilization. If Lycidas is already inaccessible, so too might be the 'Ode on the Morning of Christ's Nativity'. In previous remarks I stressed how certain generalized modes of being may be activated by a cultural reference back, but so far as knowledge is concerned, we must face the alternative possibility, that large areas of that culture may become inaccessible. Intellectual specialization will assist this process in some ways, as will the attempt to eliminate religious knowledge from the curricula of schools. Of course ignorance in this sphere has always been very great (the mediaeval priest often barely knew the Lord's Prayer), but we are faced now by an ignorance in the élite which is certainly one indication of the possibility of a secular society.

In November last I was in Cologne Cathedral with a Professor of Philosophy of a reputable university, and he turned to me to ask 'What denomination is this?' For a moment I was too stunned and embarrassed to answer, since all around us were accumulated the symbols of the Catholic faith: the shrine of the Three Kings, statues of the Virgin, the altar light, confessionals. Yet here was a highly educated, humane man, stumbling around like a befuddled barbarian in one of the major monuments of his civilization, feeling as puzzled as I would be in a Japanese temple. On the other hand, there remains an element of direct appeal about rite and ceremony which can overleap the opaque resistance brought about by ignorance. My four-year-old son is not remarkable for knowledge of anything, but on seeing a service from Exeter Cathedral on television said, 'I know why churches are true, because the people in them like singing and walk about in patterns'. He had directly apprehended two of the notae of the Church: order and ecstasy.

There is a further point that relates to the psychology of the future, since there is not simply an element of understanding required with regard to rite and symbol, but a *psychology* which makes both accessible. I refer to this only briefly because it is an area where precise prognostication about the future is impossible. The question itself can be put very simply: will the human beings of coming generations have any idea why anyone should wish to kneel, or have any wish to do the same themselves? Is a man standing on his own two feet, captain of his fate, in irreconcilable opposition to a kneeling man? Is kneeling merely the religious analogue of fear and submission in the political realm, which vanishes as soon as its political correlative disappears? Or does it express certain primal truths about an ultimate dependence, and certain quite basic emotions of awe, wonder and gratitude? May not men desire a cleansing more absolute than a psychoanalytically assisted tolerance of oneself? I do not pretend to know the answer to such questions, but I am clear that they are relevant to the possibility of a secular society. Of one thing I am reasonably certain. Having invented the therapeutic community, psycho-analysts will soon be inventing the Church, and provided nobody lets on, there will be considerable excitement in N.W.6.

In the course of reviewing certain areas of life so far, I have indicated various barriers to the achievement of complete secular-ity: the confrontation of pragmatic politics by visionary politics, the refusal to accept the disenchantment of nature, and I have also indicated various springs within our civilization from which religious awareness might be renewed. However, I ought also to say that hitherto these resistances have been fragmented, and even to some extent mutually exclusive. Experiences for which institu-tional religion once provided the central authority and link are now isolated provinces. One man finds his consolations in music, another in literature, another in the commitments of visionary politics, yet another in the countryside. The unified emotional environment within which they might make up a coherent religious approach to the world mediated by an ecclesiastical institution is no longer there. Indeed, although these things may be regarded as the secret names of God, there is no necessity to hold that this is so.

There is indeed a widespread fear both of any explicit link with the name of God and an even greater fear of any mediation through ecclesiastical institutions. Partly this is because ecclesi-astical institutions are themselves secularized in the sense that they retain links with the political authority. This is unlikely to remain permanent, but so long as it has been so both God and the Church have been suspected of doubling for social authority, and religious impulses have been partly forced into fragmented, implicit forms outside the official institutional format and the formal accepted titles of the divine. In other words the rejection of the church in the sense of unease in using its language, however sonorous and beautiful, may stem in part from a rejection of its secularized form. Religion in Britain was the first industry to be nationalized: it may be the first to be denationalized.

Thus the keystone of the institutional Church has been weakened and the great words – God, glory, holiness, praise, prayer, benediction, blessedness, have been partly compromised.

To the effects of this compromise there is added another tendency which signals a general retreat from explicitness. With the advance of science the religious man of today knows that he knows something, but he is not sure what it is (this is part of the appeal of the masterful evasiveness found in Zen). The areas where he experiences transcendence, split and divided as they are, are mute indicators, not firm proclamations. He has a kind of faith in these mute indicators, a faith which wants to rise above silence but cannot rise to the massive verbal explicitness of the Church's creed. The revolving liturgy of the countryside is too ambiguous and too implicit, the Church's creed too explicit, and therefore perhaps too easily involved in the obsolescence of the scientific views of the world with which it attempts a contemporary liaison.

The intimations of music are too vague, but the Church's heaven is all too clear and too stated, to be securely believed. Words are damaged not only by their social association but by the fact that they are words. One is caught in the paradox that if one is assailed by a great mystery it both needs to be spoken of and yet cannot be spoken. It may even be that each man may eventually have to construct for himself certain dumb partial certitudes which are his own private faith, and these will not surface in the form of visible ecclesiastical institutions. Such, at any rate, is an influential view accepted by writers like Thomas Luckmann and Robert Bellah. If this view is correct, then a secular society would be possible in the special restricted sense of a collapse of coherent world views mediated through massive institutions. As one pop star put it recently: why *should* ten million people believe the same thing?

Of course, insofar as each person constructed a personal symbolism or what Luckmann calls a 'self-steered system of relevance', religion will remain, provided you conceive the essence of religion as consisting precisely in such symbols and systems of relevance.

I would like to conclude by some critical remarks about such a view, more particularly insofar as it is put forward as a new stage to which the future will increasingly approximate. Authors like Bellah renew the life of religion by defining its fundamental characteristic as a personal, creative, individual symbolization of antinomies of man's being. That quite a considerable cultural area may illustrate this tendency I do not dispute: in any case, it already has a very long history in eastern religion. Bryan Wilson would for his part see a future for religion within the small, intimate emotional satisfactions of the small group: the sect. What I wish to say in conclusion relates to the possibility of religion surviving not only in personal poetry or the small group but within massive institutions retaining some minimal centrality in relation to the mainstream of life, culture and politics.

I can best do this by summarizing Bellah's view, since it contrasts quite sharply with my own, in spite of areas of overlap and partial agreement which it would be tedious to define precisely at this moment. It seems to me that Bellah's view rests too closely on an American experience and expresses all too clearly an extreme individualism.[1] The following points will perhaps illustrate these tendencies.

In Bellah's view, more and more people are setting light to doctrinal orthodoxy and insisting on a personal interpretation which may involve extensive personal reinterpretation. This personal approach eschews any rejection of the present mundane reality and ceases to aspire to that which is beyond the empirical world, or to withdraw from its social structures, except that it ceases to 'double for the political authority'. It explores the self and establishes man's captaincy of his soul as well as some degree of mastery of his external fate. Everyman increasingly makes and remakes himself and his worlds, in relation to the great inescapabilities of life. The religious quest can fulfil itself in so-called secular thought and art. This fluidity of the self and its symbolization is paralleled by the fluidity of religious groupings, which continually form, reform and disappear. In brief, modernity is characterized by flux, multidimensionality, individualism and this-worldliness. Hence there is a corresponding loss of institutional coherence, organic unity, common symbolism, and of any sense that here we have no abiding city. California is the future of the

[1] For a critique of individualistic interpretations see W. Stark *The Sociology of Religion* Vol. 4 (1969).

world in embryo: a kind of orgy of costless sincerity.

Now, of course Robert Bellah is too clever a sociologist not to hedge his bets about this process, but it remains the general direction as he sees it. It is also quite clear that if religion is seen as man's need to come to terms with the conditions of human life and with the reality of change, then a secular society is indeed barely possible. You *can* define religion in that way, and by the same definition eliminate the possibility of secularization. Definitions are – like comment – free, but this definition is not one I would want to use very frequently. In any case, what I want to assert at the moment is the possibility that religion may continue not only in the sense Bellah proposes, whereby indeed it has little option but to continue, but also in the sense of a continuing massive institutional presence, mediating a common symbolism and holding up though not enforcing, certain affirmations for acceptance or rejection which go beyond the empirical realities of our world. In short, I believe the Church will survive. I believe the formless can be given a form, the intimation a discipline, the categories an explicit and overall relation, the symbols a common resonance, the faith a clear and exultant voice, and the common life an abiding structure. That will be the Church, and it will be alongside *but not be superseded by* what I have elsewhere called incipient awarenesses, formless mysteries, reverences, unfocussed rejoicings, occasions which seem to point beyond themselves without explicit religious language or sacramental expression.

The religions of the world are in the final analysis only two in number: those who are the children of Abraham and who constitute the Judaeo-Christian-Islamic group, and those who belong to the Hindu-Buddhist complex of religious awareness.

What I think Bellah proposes is that the more refined enlightenment doctrines of the latter will join with a Quakerized and extremely individualistic version of the former to constitute the religion of the future. Now it may be that such syncretism will occur, supplemented no doubt by self-exploration and depth psychology. But the differences between these two traditions are so great that I am inclined to regard them as intrinsic or inherent alternatives which retain their integrity by being honestly differentiated from each other, which can only be reconciled in an analysis so much the last analysis that it would be unwise to attempt it. Their point of overlap, however interesting, is emphatically not their reconciliation, nor need we see marginal concensus between them as the religion of the future, as if the future always lay democratically half-way between two coherent alternatives.

The children of Abraham are children of history, for whom the events of history have a meaning only partially revealed in history. That meaning turns on an axial period in history and on a goal of history, which is again a goal only in a limited sense *within* the historical process. This meaning derives from a source who is in a profound sense other than man as well as most intimately with him. He is the focus of salvation for all mankind, greatest and least, sophisticated and totally unenlightened, through faith. This faith is both personal commitment and an acceptance of certain basic affirmations about what is ultimately real, the nature and destiny of man. This gives religion a common focal symbolism, a 'solid poetry', which however much personally interpreted, retains it centrality. Those who reject these affirmations and cannot make this commitment are outside the household of faith, which has structure, form, continuity, norms and criteria for the definition of truth and falsehood.

For Christianity at least, the norm is defined by a particular person: monotheism with a human face. By turning the eyes of faith on to history and the external world, this tradition is both a preparation for science including the science of history, and vulnerable to its findings. The Christian tradition also turns on 'a sense of tragedy inseparable from the mystery of injustice, from the conviction that man is a precarious guest in a world where forces of unreason have grim licence!' Nothing in our modern experience seems to me seriously to wean us from this conviction.

For the alternative tradition, the soul is central, and history and time devalued. In some variants the material world itself is but an illusion. Thus, there is much less vulnerability to history and to science. Since there is no focal, axial point, there is no common symbolism, though certain stories are useful and important 'provisional means'. A story or poetic symbol merely illustrates a universal principle, and it is not plagued by the supposed scandal of particularity. Private poetry may achieve infinite symbolic proliferation, and by the same token religious groupings may proliferate and reform without clearly defined centre or organic continuity. The crucial differentiation is not between believer and unbeliever, but between the enlightened and the mass of unenlightened, that is, it is horizontal and not vertical. Clearly, such a religious tradition is close to Bellah's view of the future, and has never contained the dynamic of secularization in the western manner, because the contrast is not fully explicit in the first place.

I have already said that these are inherent alternatives with different losses and gains attached to each, but it is worth pointing out that so far as the immediate future is concerned, a violently exclusive secular version of the western tradition is sweeping large areas of the eastern cultural region, and is very far from embodying the likelihood of free personal symbolization. Marxism is a religion of the book, overwhelmingly verbal in its expression, with a sharp sense of truth and falsehood, of either/or, aided by a doctrine of axial history and the goal of history. It has norms and criteria defining its central tradition, creating a continuous, firmly directed structure, and at the same time it defines schisms and heresies. Marxism recovers with dramatic and alarming strength, the ability of the mediaeval church to monopolize the symbolism and doctrinal orthodoxy of a culture. Not merely does it 'double for the political authority': it *is* it. Even California may seem preferable by comparison, but extant Marxist cultures provide an alternative model of a future dominated by a 'secular' variant of western religion which I'm not inclined to ignore. The political analogue of mediaeval certainties is clearly with us.

When I say I believe the Church will survive, I do not mean, of course, that it will recover those monopolistic, centralized certainties, so characteristic of the modern Marxist Churches, whether their Vatican is in Third Rome, or in Peking. And I have made it plain that I think the development of syncretism between the individualistic deposit of Protestantism and eastern religion will occur on a fairly large scale. But in our western tradition, the word has not only been made explicit but made flesh; in Carlyle's phrase, it is embodied in a 'speaking man', and it divides with some clarity those who unite in its affirmations from those who are honestly agnostic and atheist. Those affirmations and rejections will not be evaded by wriggling down some bolthole of personal exploration and depth psychology, or by attempting to define the atheist in.

Perhaps in some manner the inner and the outer, explicit word and variable symbol, poetic truth and truthful poetry, personal symbolization and objective verity are reconcilable, but they are still sharply and intrinsically different, and I see no reason why the religion of the future should embody only one of them. In a way I could call it a choice between Yeats and Eliot as prophets of the modern world. For Yeats, all the various symbol systems were merely 'provisional means' to personal truth. For Eliot too, there was a realization that words slip, slide and strain, but also a trusting of the word, its explicit promises, and the community it creates.